PENGUIN  CLASSICS

LA VITA NUOVA

DANTE ALIGHIERI was born in Florence in 1265 and belonged to a noble but impoverished family. He followed a normal course of studies, possibly attending university in Bologna, and when he was about twenty he married Gemma Donati, by whom he had three children. He had first met Bice Portinari, whom he called Beatrice, in 1274, and when she died in 1290 he sought distraction by studying philosophy and theology and by writing the *Vita Nuova*. During this time he became involved in the strife between the Guelfs and the Ghibellines; he became a prominent White Guelf and when the Black Guelfs came to power in 1302 Dante, during an absence from Florence, was condemned to exile. He took refuge first in Verona and after wandering from place to place, possibly to Paris and even, some have said improbably, to Oxford, he settled in Ravenna. While there he completed *The Divine Comedy*, which he had begun in about 1308, if not later. Dante died in Ravenna in 1321.

BARBARA REYNOLDS was for twenty-two years Lecturer in Italian at Cambridge University and subsequently Reader in Italian Studies at Nottingham University. Her first book was a textual reconstruction of the linguistic writings of Alessandro Manzoni. The General Editor of the *Cambridge Italian Dictionary*, she was created Cavaliere Ufficiale al Merito della Repubblica Italiana in 1978. She has been awarded silver medals by the Italian Government and by the Province of Vicenza and the Edmund Gardner Prize for her services to Italian scholarship. She has been Visiting Professor at the University of California, Berkeley, at Wheaton College, Illinois, at Hope College, Michigan, and at Trinity College, Dublin. She has translated Dante's *Paradiso*, left unfinished by Dorothy L. Sayers on her death in 1957, and Ariosto's *Orlando Furioso* for the Penguin Classics. She is the author of *The Passionate Intellect: Dorothy L. Sayers' Encounter with Dante* and *Dorothy L. Sayers: Her Life and Soul*. She is also the editor of *The Letters of Dorothy L. Sayers*. She holds three Honorary Doctorates and is the managing editor of *SEVEN: An Anglo-American Literary Review*.

DANTE ALIGHIERI

La Vita Nuova

(Poems of Youth)

Translated with an Introduction by
BARBARA REYNOLDS

REVISED EDITION

PENGUIN BOOKS

PENGUIN BOOKS

Published by the Penguin Group
Penguin Books Ltd, 80 Strand, London WC2R ORL, England
Penguin Group (USA) Inc., 375 Hudson Street, New York, New York 10014, USA
Penguin Books Australia Ltd, 250 Camberwell Road, Camberwell, Victoria 3124, Australia
Penguin Books Canada Ltd, 10 Alcorn Avenue, Toronto, Ontario, Canada M4V 3B2
Penguin Books India (P) Ltd, 11 Community Centre, Panchsheel Park, New Delhi – 110 017, India
Penguin Books (NZ) Ltd, Cnr Rosedale and Airborne Roads, Albany, Auckland, New Zealand
Penguin Books (South Africa) (Pty) Ltd, 24 Sturdee Avenue, Rosebank 2196, South Africa

Penguin Books Ltd, Registered Offices: 80 Strand, London WC2R ORL, England

www.penguin.com

This translation first published 1969
Revised edition, 2004

8

Copyright © Barbara Reynolds, 1969, 2004
All rights reserved

Set in 10.25/12.25 pt PostScript Adobe Sabon
Typeset by Rowland Phototypesetting Ltd, Bury St Edmunds, Suffolk
Printed in England by Clays Ltd, St Ives plc

ISBN-13: 978-0-140-44947-1

www.greenpenguin.co.uk

Penguin Books is committed to a sustainable future
for our business, our readers and our planet.
The book in your hands is made from paper
certified by the Forest Stewardship Council.

Contents

LA VITA NUOVA

Foreword to the Revised Edition

Over thirty years have passed since my translation of the *Vita Nuova* was first published by Penguin Classics in 1969. It has been reprinted many times and has met with a measure of acceptance. Since then I have altered some of my views on the work and in the course of writing a biography of Dante I have made one or two discoveries. I have accordingly provided a new Introduction and made a few adjustments to the Notes. There are also some alterations to the verse.

Cambridge, 2003

Chronology

(From the birth of Dante to his entry into political life)*

1265 between 21 May and 21 June: Birth of Dante.

1266 January: Birth of Beatrice.

1274 traditionally 1 May: First meeting of Dante and Beatrice.

1280–82 Dante composes and circulates his earliest sonnets.

1283 1 May: Second meeting of Dante and Beatrice. May–June: Dante's father has died by this date and Dante comes of age, at eighteen, as an orphan, according to the laws of Florence. May–June?: Dante composes and circulates a sonnet describing a dream (the first sonnet in *La Vita Nuova*). Meeting with Guido Cavalcanti and beginning of their friendship. Dante affects love for the first screen-lady.

1284 Dante composes a *serventese* containing the names of the sixty most beautiful women in Florence.

(1284? Marriage of Dante to Gemma Donati.)

1285? Departure from Florence of first screen-love.

1285 Autumn: Death of a friend of Beatrice. October: Dante takes part in cavalry expedition of Florentine militia in support of Tuscan Guelfs against the Castle of Poggio di Santa Cecilia, which, roused to rebellion by the Ghibellines of Arezzo, surrendered in April 1286.

1286 April–May?: Dante pays court to the second screen-love. Beatrice snubs him.

(1289 11 June: Dante takes part in the Battle of Campaldino against the Ghibellines of Arezzo. August: Dante takes part in the siege of Caprona, near Pisa.)

---

* All events, except those in parentheses, are mentioned in or deduced from *La Vita Nuova*. The dates are not all certain.

1289 31 December: Death of Beatrice's father, Folco dei Portinari.

1290 January: Illness of Dante. 8 June: Death of Beatrice. Summer: Visit to Dante of Beatrice's brother.

1291 8 June: First anniversary of death of Beatrice; some men of importance visit Dante as he draws figures of angels.

1292? Dante first sees the compassionate young woman (the 'donna gentile') looking at him from a window.

1293? Vision of Beatrice as a child.

1293 Easter?: Pilgrims pass through Florence on their way to Rome.

1293? Vision of Beatrice in Heaven.

(**1294?** Composition of *La Vita Nuova*.

1295 Dante enters political life.)

Introduction

The *Vita Nuova* is a treatise by a poet, written for poets, on the
art of poetry. It consists of a selection of Dante's early poems –
a selection he made himself – combined with his own prose
commentary. The commentary is of two kinds. First, Dante
narrates the events and emotions which led him to compose
each poem; then, unless he considers that the meaning has
already been made sufficiently clear, he analyses the relationship
of the content to the structure.

The majority of the poems are directly concerned with Dante's
love for Beatrice, and all of them have some bearing on this
theme. He does not divulge her family name but she has been
identified with Beatrice, the daughter of a prominent Florentine
citizen, Folco dei Portinari. She was one of eleven children, five
sons and six daughters. One of her brothers was a close friend
of Dante. Folco dei Portinari held government office and was
elected Prior of Florence in August 1282. In 1288 he founded
the Hospital of Santa Maria Nuova. In his will, dated 15 January
1288, it is shown that Beatrice, to whom he bequeathed fifty
Florentine pounds, was by then married to Simone dei Bardi, a
member of a prominent family of bankers. She died in 1290,
aged twenty-four. A few years later, possibly between 1292 and
1294, when he was in his late twenties, perhaps in an attempt
to recover from his grief, Dante assembled his poems and wrote
his commentaries.

The title, translated literally, means 'New Life', but it is not
certain that Dante originally intended it to be the title of the
whole work. It arises from the Latin words *incipit vita nova*
('here begins the new life'), which Dante says stand near the

beginning of his 'book of memory'. It may therefore have been meant only as an introduction to the first few chapters which cover his childhood. There are at least two later indications in the work that other headings were intended. The Latin adjective *novus* means not only 'new' but also 'first', 'inexperienced', 'untried'; it can also mean 'wonderful', 'marvellous', 'unheard-of'. The Italian phrase *vita nuova* does not occur anywhere in the text itself, but Dante refers to it with that title in *Il Convivio* ('The Banquet'), a philosophical work he wrote in the early years of his exile.[1] The phrase is used again, though ambiguously, in *Purgatorio*, where Beatrice, speaking of Dante to the angels, says that grace

> . . . had so endowed this man potentially,
> in his new life that from such gifts as those
> a wondrous harvest should have come to be.[2]

In this context the phrase seems to mean youth, or it may be an allusion to the work itself. Whatever the explanation, an element of novelty, of things discovered and untried, is certainly a feature of the *Vita Nuova*.

When Dante was about seventeen he began sending copies of his poems to other poets, as was the custom at the time. One of his earliest was a sonnet describing a dream (later the first poem in the *Vita Nuova*), in which Love appears in the conventional figure of a *signore* ('master or lord'). He has Dante's heart in his hand and in his arms he holds a sleeping woman, naked except for a crimson mantle cast loosely about her. Among the poets who replied was Dante of Maiano, who took a coarse, rollicking tone and, in what seems a parody of medical advice, told his young namesake to give his testicles a good wash to see if that would clear his head; if not, he suggested he should see a doctor and present a specimen of his urine. A serious reply came from a distinguished poet, Guido Cavalcanti, Dante's senior by about ten years and the most eminent among the poetic group to which Dante hoped to be admitted. It was the beginning of an important friendship, of which the *Vita Nuova* was the direct outcome.

As soon as he came under the influence of Cavalcanti, Dante's range extended and his skill developed. His earliest poems had been sonnets, of no particular originality. On Cavalcanti's advice he tried his hand at the *canzone*, a form derived from the Provençal *canso*, a poem intended to be sung, as the word indicates. The structure was elaborate and in strict accordance with musical form. He also experimented with the *ballata* (a form of verse designed to be accompanied by a dance as well as sung).

The Italian vernacular was then scarcely 150 years old and only about half a century old as a literary language. Cavalcanti and his Florentine circle were on the brink of uncharted waters as they discussed the potential of this new, untried language. Snatches of conversation between him and Dante can be heard in the prose of the *Vita Nuova*. Discussing the question of personification, Dante says that since the Latin poets used it, there is no reason why it should not also be used in vernacular rhyme, though never as a mere ornament. It must always be possible to reveal the true meaning that lies beneath:

> I will add that the Latin poets did not write in this manner without good reason, nor should those who compose in rhyme, if they cannot justify what they say; for it would be a disgrace if someone composing in rhyme introduced a figure of speech or rhetorical ornament, and then on being asked could not divest his words of such covering so as to reveal a true meaning. My most intimate friend and I know quite a number who compose rhymes in this stupid manner. (Chapter XXV)

Not only is the *Vita Nuova* the outcome of such conversations. There is more than one hint that the work was written in accordance with Cavalcanti's wishes. Dante says, for instance, that when Beatrice died he wrote a lament in Latin, but he does not include it because it was his intention to write the work only in Italian, and he adds:

> I am well aware, too, that my closest friend, for whom I write this work, also desired that I should write it entirely in the vernacular. (Chapter XXX)

These words have been taken to mean that Dante dedicated his book to Cavalcanti. They may not bear such a formal significance, but it is clear that his 'first friend' was at his elbow as he wrote. Even so, Dante does not entirely dispense with the senior language. The book begins and ends with a Latin phrase and there are quotations from the Vulgate and classical authors in the course of the text. Dante's faculties, personified as 'spirits' (a concept he borrowed from Cavalcanti) and the personified figure of Love address him in Latin, as though the vernacular were not solemn or venerable enough for such high and significant converse.

By the time Beatrice died Dante was recognized in Florence as a leading poet. His verses were sung, recited and memorized, not only by men, as at first, but also by women, some of whom commissioned him to write for them. He had achieved a public. He also knew he had ventured into new territory. In the beginning, like his Florentine friends, he had written within the conventions inherited from the troubadours and their Sicilian and Italian imitators. The stock situations were: the torment of unrequited love, the obligation to keep secret the name of the beloved, the device of a 'screen-love' to deceive the inquisitive, the personification of Death as a pitiless destroyer of youth, misunderstandings with the beloved, intolerable ecstasy in her presence and anguished mortification at her mockery. A new ingredient had recently been added by a poet of Bologna, Guido Guinizelli, who created the concept of the *cor gentile* ('gentle, or noble heart'), a quality of mind and soul which alone made it possible to experience the elevating effect of love.

The avant-garde poets who gathered round Cavalcanti saw themselves as an in-group who had special understanding of this concept. They may have met in Cavalcanti's house, bringing their latest compositions to be read aloud or more probably sung. Their poems may also have been expounded and discussed. In which case, the prose sections of the *Vita Nuova* may be a development of such gatherings, which were probably in the nature of concerts or recitals. When a poet sent a composition to his lady the occasion must have been similar to an *aubade* or a serenade. How such performances were organized, whether they were public or private, whether the singers, or in the case of a *ballata*, the dancers, were paid professionals or amateurs are questions which have not been investigated. We do know the name of one of the singers: it is Casella, whose soul Dante encounters on the shore of the Mountain of Purgatory and whose singing, Dante says, was a solace to his pangs of love. At Dante's request, he sings once more, probably to music which he had himself composed, one of Dante's own *canzoni*. Dante and Virgil, together with a group of other newly arrived souls, listen enraptured.

The love life of the group of poets with whom Dante mingled ranged beyond the idealized vision of one woman. It is easy to forget that they led everyday lives, pursued their professions, took part in politics, attended social functions, met and courted attractive women, married and had love affairs. Guido Caval-canti and a fellow poet Lapo Gianni, who were both married, shared the same mistress. Like the others, they separated their real from their imaginative lives, in which the experience of love, analysed in terms of new concepts, underwent a process of spiritualization. But not all their poems were written in this mode.

In a charming and subtly erotic sonnet Dante expresses a wish that he and Guido and Lapo Gianni might sail away together in a boat, accompanied by three women whom they love: Giov-anna (for Guido), Lagia (for Lapo) and, for himself, 'she who is number thirty on the list'. We do not know her name but it is certainly not Beatrice:

> Guido, I wish you, I and Lapo could,
> by virtue of enchantment, taken be
> and placed upon a boat, to sail the sea,
> no matter what the wind, where'er we would.
> And that no tempest or ill-omened flood
> might put our voyaging in jeopardy,
> but, living ever in such harmony,
> we'd find our pleasure day by day renewed.

And that the kind magician might convey
Giovanna, Lagia in the boat with us,
with her who's number thirty in my rhyme.
Then in Love's converse we would spend our time,
making all three content and bounteous,
while we, I vow, would joyful be as they.[3]

This sonnet is not included in the *Vita Nuova*, but he does mention a poem (no longer extant) in which he listed the names of the sixty most beautiful women of Florence. The name of Beatrice coincided with the number nine, which as the square of the Trinity signified a mystical quality attaching to her, not her position in a beauty contest. Indeed he says elsewhere in the same work that her loveliness was like a miracle beyond compare.

Dante recounts that he first set eyes on Beatrice in childhood, when she was just turned eight and he was nearly nine. He recalls that she was dressed in 'a decorous and delicate crimson, tied with a girdle and trimmed in a manner suited to her tender age' (Chapter II). It is Boccaccio, the first biographer of Dante, who said that the meeting took place at a May Day party in the house of Beatrice's father. Looking back on the occasion Dante says that he became aware that he then fell in love with her and thought of her as angelic, endowed with divine qualities, noble and praiseworthy in all her ways. He often went where he could see her, even during his boyhood, but she does not seem to have spoken directly to him, or in a way which had particular meaning for him, until nine years later. Then one day he saw her, dressed in white, walking along a street in Florence, in the company of two older women. She turned and greeted him. Her greeting filled him with intense joy and he withdrew to his room to think about her. Falling asleep he had (or so he says) the dream which is the subject of the first sonnet (Chapter III).[4]

From then onwards Dante's thoughts dwelt constantly on Beatrice, so much so that his health began to suffer and his friends grew concerned about him. He admitted that it was love that had thus reduced him but he declined to reveal the name of the one he loved. The society in which he moved was small and closely knit. People took a keen interest in each other's affairs and there was much gossip. He describes being in church one day, sitting where he could gaze at Beatrice, who was also present. Another woman, who sat in his line of vision, thought he was gazing at her and this gave him the idea of making her his 'screen-love', to deceive those who were taking too much interest in him. The scene is not difficult to imagine: the other woman who in her vanity thought that Dante was looking at her, the friends who thought so too, the nudges and the raised eyebrows, the chatter and laughter as they came out of church. Not much attention can have been paid to the sermon that day.

The 'screen-love's' delusion must have been confirmed by the poems which Dante wrote for her. Possibly it was not a delusion. He says that her appearance was very pleasing and that when she left Florence he was more dismayed than he would have believed possible. Eventually he replaced her by another 'screen-love'. His way of narrating this is figurative. He says that he was riding on a journey with a company of people, in the direction of the region where his 'screen-love' now lived. Along the way he met Love dressed in humble travelling clothes, who advised him to take a new 'screen-love' and mentioned her name. On his return to Florence he played the part of her admirer so ardently that malicious gossip reached the ears of Beatrice, who cut him in the street.

The snub upset Dante deeply. He fled to the privacy of his room where he lay on his bed and wept, falling asleep 'like a little child that has been beaten' (Chapter XII). In his sleep he dreamt that Love stood beside him in the figure of a young man dressed in white. He gazed pensively at Dante, then, sighing, spoke to him in Latin, saying, 'My son, it is time for our false images to be put aside.' He then wept and when Dante asked him why, he said, again in Latin, 'I am like the centre of a circle, to which the parts of the circumference are related in similar manner; you, however, are not.' When Dante asked what these words meant, Love replied, in the vernacular, 'Do not ask more than is useful for you.' He then explained why Beatrice had withdrawn her greeting: his attentions to the new 'screen-love' had given rise to scandal and she feared her own name might suffer likewise.

Since Dante's secret was already partly known to Beatrice, Love advised him to write a poem addressed indirectly to her, saying that he had loved her ever since boyhood and that when his gaze rested on another woman Love made him see in her face the face of Beatrice: 'In this way she will come to know your true desire and will see how mistaken are the words of those who speak wrongly about you' (Chapter XII). He is to take special care that the poem is set to harmonious music. Since it is to be a *ballata*, it will be danced as well as sung.

This imaginary dialogue between himself and the figure of Love represents Dante's guilt and embarrassment. He has been indiscreet in his affair with the new 'screen-love'; he knows that he has been deceiving himself in pretending that his love is always pure and ennobling, though he believes that there is a perfect state of mind and soul in which all love is good; he has an inkling that it is a question of ideal relationship, such as that of the mid-point of a circle, but he is a long way from understanding it. He personifies the *ballata*, bidding it seek the company of Love. Together they are to visit Beatrice and ask her forgiveness. When she has heard the song, Love is to explain the reasons for Dante's apparent love of other women. Beneath the complex poetic figure we glimpse a picture of Beatrice receiving the dancers and singers into her home or perhaps her garden, watching and listening to them.

From an event which followed soon afterwards it does not seem that she was much moved. A friend invited Dante to accompany him to a wedding reception. Among the guests was Beatrice. He sensed her presence even before he saw her and became so faint that he had to lean 'for support against a fresco painted in a frieze round the walls of the house' (Chapter XIV). This was observed by other women who laughed at him and Beatrice too joined in their mockery. He was so overcome that he thought he was dying. His friend had to take him by the hand and lead him away. He returned to his room, where again he wept in an agony of shame. It occurred to him that if he explained to Beatrice why the sight of her so overwhelmed him she might have compassion on him. Although it was contrary to convention to do so, he now addressed three sonnets directly to her. The first of these, reproaching her for her mockery, begins:

> With your companions you make fun of me,
>   Not thinking, Lady, what the reason is
>   I cut so strange a figure in your eyes
>   When, raising mine, your loveliness I see.
>   If you but knew, Pity no more could be
>   Severe towards me in her usual guise.
>   Finding me near you, Love his weapons tries,
>   Gaining in boldness and temerity. (Chapter XIV)

Later, a group of women, perhaps those who had mocked him at the wedding, asked him what the point of his love was, since he was so overcome in his lady's presence. He replied that his joy originally lay in her greeting but now that this was denied him he found all his beatitude in writing in praise of her. One of the women retorted: 'If you were telling the truth, those words you have composed to describe your state would have been written in such a way as to convey a different meaning' (Chapter XVIII). With feminine directness, she had put her finger on the nub: all his poems up to then had been self-pitying laments. The conversation suggests that Dante may have met with a similar challenge at one of the poetry recitals.

Thinking the matter over, he realized that the women were right: the time had come for him to concentrate in his poems on the beauty and virtue of Beatrice and leave aside his sufferings. But the more he thought about it, the more afraid he was to begin, as though he were standing on the edge of an undertaking that might prove beyond his powers. One day, as he walked by a stream of very clear water, his tongue, as though moved of its own accord, uttered the words:

Donne ch'avete intelletto d'amore[5] (Chapter XIX)

These words seemed to him an excellent beginning for a poem, as well as for the new direction he wished to take. He stored them away in his mind for several days until he found the resolve to continue. The completed poem is the first *canzone* in the *Vita Nuova* and ushers in what have been called the poems of praise.

There was nothing new in poems of praise. This was a very usual theme in the poetry of the time. What is different is that the imaginative transformation of Dante's experience of love had entered a new stage. Beatrice was now more than the focus of a conventional, poeticized love. In thinking of writing poems in praise of her he came to realize that she represented something beyond herself: ideal virtue, incomparable beauty, a paradisiacal being for whose presence in Heaven the angels and the saints were clamouring. This is Dante's first step towards a new form of allegory: it is not personification or symbolism, but the perception that actual persons can be images of qualities beyond themselves. This would immensely enlarge his range, leading eventually to the creation of allegorical figures which are also convincing characters in the *Divine Comedy*.

Years later, when he was two-thirds of the way through his major work, Dante looked back to this *canzone* and recognized it as a turning point. In *Purgatorio*, on the cornice of the gluttons, he introduces the soul of the poet Bonagiunta of Lucca, to whom he gives the following words:

> 'But say, do I see here the man who wove
> the strands of those new verses which begin,
> *Ladies who understanding have of love?*'

Dante replies:

> 'I am the one who when
> Love breathes in me, take note, and in the way
> that he dictates I say what he does mean.'[6]

Bonagiunta answers: 'Oh, now I see what is meant by what they call the *dolce stil nuovo*.'

This Italian phrase has always been translated into English as 'sweet new style', but that is not what it means. In Italian, as in French, when there are two or more adjectives it is the final one which carries the emphasis. In English, this is the function of the first adjective. The point is that there was already a *dolce stile* ('sweet style'), as there was also an *aspro stile* ('harsh style'). What Dante had initiated was a *new* sweet style.

Not all Dante's fellow poets were so perceptive or so admiring. Dante of Maiano was not the only one who mocked him. Cecco Angiolieri, who wrote comic verse, teased him about a contradiction in one of his sonnets. Dante did not expect (or even want) many of his readers to understand him, nor did he always take himself as solemnly as some of his commentators have done. He wrote some teasing lines to a certain Brunetto Brunelleschi about a poem he knew would be beyond his wits. In another sonnet he makes fun of himself for absent-mindedly gazing up at Carisenda, the leaning tower in Bologna, oblivious of what was going on around him. A delightful tease, seldom if ever mentioned by Dante scholars, occurred in the eighteenth century when Lorenzo da Ponte (who was well read in Italian literature) wrote his charming parody of '*Donne ch'avete intelletto d'amore*' in the words he gives to the lovesick Cherubino to sing to 'his' ladies in *Le Nozze di Figaro* ('The Marriage of Figaro'):

> Voi che sapete che cosa è amor . . .[7]

When Dante's *canzone* had been heard by several people, a friend asked him to write a poem defining love. To do so he had recourse to a definition already provided by the predecessor from whom he and his friends acknowledged derivation, namely Guido Guinizelli of Bologna. He does not give his name but calls him *il saggio* ('the wise man') and quotes his concept of the 'noble heart':

> Love and the noble heart are but one thing,
>   Even as the wise man tells us in his rhyme,
>   The one without the other venturing
>   No more than reason from a reasoning mind.

> Nature, disposed to love, creates Love king,
> Making the heart a dwelling-place for him
> Wherein he lies quiescent, slumbering
> Sometimes a little, now a longer time.
> Then beauty in a virtuous woman's face
> Pleases the eyes, striking the heart so deep
> A yearning for the pleasing thing may rise.
> Sometimes so long it lingers in that place
> Love's spirit is awakened from his sleep.
> By a worthy man a woman's moved likewise.
> (Chapter XX)

What Beatrice felt about Dante and his idealization of her we can only guess. Perhaps it was a matter of gratification, both to her and her husband, that she should be the focus of the outstanding devotion of so admired a poet. We first see her as an adult walking down a street in Florence, dressed in white, chaperoned by two older women; she turns on noticing Dante and greets him graciously. Next she is offended by the excessive attention he pays to another woman and we see the scornful toss of her head as she cuts him in the street. Then we find her laughing unkindly with other women at his trembling embarrassment in her presence. In a sonnet, not included in the *Vita Nuova*, we see her among a group of beautiful women, she the most beautiful of them all, when Dante dares to look directly in her face and sees an image of an angel. Wherever she goes she inspires virtue. Her greeting, when she is disposed to grant it, bestows salvation and fills him with love of the whole world. In one sonnet he describes his happiness on seeing her walking behind Giovanna, also known as Primavera, whom Cavalcanti loved, and in the commentary he interprets the occasion as a revelation of St John the Baptist, who will come first (*prima verrà*), followed by Christ. By the time he wrote the commentary his perception of the natural as an image of the supernatural had reached an advanced stage. To understand how Beatrice was related to this image, he resolved to devote himself to a period of study and reflection, in order, as he says at the end of the work, to prepare himself to write of Beatrice 'what has never been written in rhyme of any woman'.

As to Beatrice's appearance, Dante says that her complexion was pearl-like, but not pale to excess. In *Purgatorio* he refers to her eyes as *smeraldi* ('emeralds'). If this means that her eyes were green, then it may be that her hair was auburn. This would account for the pale skin which is a feature of people with reddish hair. He says that she was devout and had a profound veneration for the Virgin Mary. We do not know where she was educated: most probably by nuns at a convent school. When her father died she was deeply grieved, although she was by then married and had left her family home. We do not know if she had children and it is possible that she died in childbirth. Dante says only that she suffered no chill or fever; she simply died suddenly.

In the prose which follows the third *canzone* he says that he does not intend to discuss *la sua partita da noi* ('her departure from us'). This has usually been interpreted as referring to her death, but this cannot be right for he then goes on to speak of it at some length. What he must mean is that he does not intend to write of her *funeral*. He gives three reasons for this: first, it is outside the subject of his book, secondly he does not possess adequate words to speak of it, and thirdly to do so would involve him in self-praise.

Funerals were very public affairs and the mourning for a beautiful young woman, whose father had been renowned, whose husband was also an eminent citizen, must have been widespread. Dante, the distinguished poet, whose poems to her were so much admired, and who was a close friend of one of her brothers, would have been an honoured guest, perhaps even one of the chief mourners. It is possible even that the lament in Latin which he says he wrote after her death may have been read out at her funeral. To have spoken of this would indeed have been to speak in praise of himself.

His grief at the death of Beatrice was overwhelming. He made no attempt to conceal it; on the contrary he deliberately made it public and seemed to take comfort in the fact that people were concerned at his forlorn aspect. He had reached the stage where the merest glance of sympathy set him weeping again, when he caught sight of a beautiful woman looking at him from a window with every appearance of compassion.

He never names this woman, probably because at the time of writing she was still alive; she is referred to simply as *la donna gentile* ('the gracious lady'). He found himself drawn more and more to her; he wrote sonnets to her, expressing the mingled consolation and accentuation of grief which her sympathy caused in him. Gradually he began to take so much pleasure in the sight of her that he reproached himself for infidelity to the memory of Beatrice. Confusion and conflict arose in him; he conversed with himself as to the nature of this new attachment. It must be, he thought, a very noble love, but in arguing within himself about this he declared that his heart was the enemy of his reason.[8] Finally he had a vision of Beatrice as a child, as he first saw her. The effect of this was to bring on fresh fits of weeping, so that his eyes became ringed with dark red patches; but the crisis, it seems, was over.

Making no transition in the narrative, Dante next relates that he saw pilgrims one day passing through Florence on their way to Rome to see the veil of St Veronica. They seemed to him absorbed in their own thoughts and unaware of the grievous loss which Florence had suffered. He felt moved, therefore, to address to them a sonnet on the subject.

The last sonnet of the *Vita Nuova* was written, Dante says, for two women of noble lineage who had sent word asking him to send them some examples of his poetry. The sonnet is an account of a vision of Beatrice in Heaven, apprehended only in part, for 'our intellect in the presence of those blessed souls is as weak as our eyes before the sun' (Chapter XLI).

It is after this sonnet that Dante, according to his account, experienced a marvellous vision which made him resolve to write no more poetry concerning Beatrice until he could do so in a manner worthy of the things he had seen. And the work concludes with the famous undertaking to study to this end so that he may 'compose concerning her what has never been written in rhyme of any woman' (Chapter XLII).

There is a difficulty about the end. In *Il Convivio* Dante interprets the *donna gentile* as philosophy. He does not deny, however, that she was a real woman. This is another example of perceiving an actual person as an image of something beyond his or her self. He says that she (that is, philosophy) replaced Beatrice and that this can be confirmed by reference to the end of the *Vita Nuova*. This has given rise to an unresolved dispute and it has even been suggested that there were two versions of the *Vita Nuova* and that in *Il Convivio* Dante was alluding to an earlier one, which has been lost, in which the *donna gentile* was shown to have replaced Beatrice. The difficulty can be solved, however, if we understand that in *Il Convivio* Dante is referring to his decision to put off writing poems about Beatrice (as in fact he did) until he had completed a period of study. In other words, it is not a question of one woman replacing another, but of one activity (the writing of poems about Beatrice) being replaced by another activity (the study of philosophy), which in fact took place.

Some readers resent and many skip those sections of the commentary in which Dante indicates the divisions of the poems, feeling such schematic analysis to be an intrusion into the dreamlike world of ecstatic love which is conjured up by the consecrated tone of the rest of the work. It is said that Dante Gabriel Rossetti, through whose translation of the *Vita Nuova* (and through whose paintings) Dante and Beatrice may be said to have become part of the Pre-Raphaelite movement, so disliked the paragraphs in which the poems are analysed that he asked his brother William to translate them for him. These analytical sections are an example of what was known as a *divisio textus*, a division of the text into parts according to content. What is intriguing is that these divisions do not correspond to the formal structure of the poems, but to the subject, which follows a separate development. It may be that Dante intended the divisions to be a guide to those who read the poems aloud, or to composers who set them to music. Whatever their function, they are an important part of the structure of the work.

The arrangement of the *Vita Nuova* is based on an elaborate pattern, of which the number nine (the square of three, the symbol of the Trinity) is the key. The thirty-one poems are placed in the following sequence: 10 short poems, 1 *canzone*, 4 short poems, 1 *canzone*, 4 short poems, 1 *canzone*, 10 short poems. The mid-point of this series is the second *canzone*. With its supporting eight short poems, four preceding, four following, it is the centre of a central group of nine. This central group is flanked by two integers, which are in turn flanked by two tens, thus:

$$10 + 1 + 9 + 1 + 10$$

which can also be arranged as:

$$1 + 9 + 1 + 9 + 1 + 9 + 1$$

in which the number nine occurs three times.

The second *canzone* is the central panel of a triptych, of which the first and third *canzoni* are the supporting panels to the left and right. This can be taken to signify the division of Dante's life into two parts, the period before Beatrice's death and the period after it. The pattern is further emphasized by a bilateral symmetry in which the early life of Beatrice at the beginning is mirrored by her celestial nature at the end. The mirror-imaging is further managed by the position of the analyses of the poems, which before Beatrice's death follow them and after her death precede them, in order, Dante says, that the poems may seem more 'widowed'.

The fascination with numerical pattern was characteristic not only of Dante but of his contemporaries. The meaning of numbers was understood to be fundamental to the study of cosmology. By understanding the virtue of numbers, the relationship between them, their squares and their cubes and what is known as mystic addition,[9] it was possible to see that the same mathematical laws governed all life. In making a work of art it was necessary to employ a numerological symbolism in order to control the relationship of its parts to the whole. Such patterns of thought were inherited from Pythagoras and preserved for the Middle Ages by St Augustine and Martianus

Capella, among others. The doctrine of the Trinity made Christian writers eager to look for patterns of three throughout creation and to construct their works according to a triple pattern. What is unique in Dante is the extraordinary skill he would eventually show in applying such control to the construction of the *Divine Comedy*.

Cambridge, January 2003

NOTES

1. Book II, chapter 2.
2. *Purgatorio*, Canto XXX, 115–17. Translation by Dorothy L. Sayers, in *The Divine Comedy: Hell, Purgatory, Paradise* (Penguin, 1949–62).
3. Translation by Barbara Reynolds. *Dante's Lyric Poetry*, Volume 1 (Clarendon Press, 1967).
4. It is unlikely that the first sonnet was written with reference to any particular woman. This is probably an example of the way in which Dante uses the commentary to adjust some of the early poems to the theme of Beatrice.
5. Rendered by Rossetti, 'Ladies who have intelligence in love'.
6. *Purgatorio*, Canto XXIV, 49–54. The line '*Ladies who understanding have of love*' is translated in this edition of the *Vita Nuova* as 'Ladies who know by insight what Love is'. (See Note 5.)
7. You who know what love is . . . *Le Nozze di Figaro*, Act II.
8. Not that the *donna gentile* was the enemy of reason, as has often been wrongly interpreted.
9. e.g. 19 = 1 + 9 = 10.

Canzone: Italian lyrical poem
↪ each word that appears
@ the end of a line of
1st stanza appears @ end
of one of lines in
following stanza

Further Reading

Vita Nuova, the Italian text, edited by Jennifer Petrie and June Salmons, with Introduction, Notes, Glossary and Vocabulary (Belfield Italian Library, 1994).

Dante's Lyric Poetry, the Italian text, edited by K. Foster and P. Boyde, with English translation and commentary, 2 vols. (Clarendon Press, 1967).

The Odes of Dante, the Italian text, edited by H. S. Vere-Hodge, with English translation and commentary (Clarendon Press, 1963).

The Divine Comedy: Hell, Purgatory, Paradise, translated by Dorothy L. Sayers, completed by Barbara Reynolds, with Introduction, Commentary and Notes, 3 vols. (Penguin, 1949–62).

Barbi, M., *Life of Dante*, translated by P. Ruggiers (University of California Press, 1966).

Boyde, P., *Dante's Style in His Lyric Poetry* (Cambridge University Press, 1971).

Jacoff, R. (ed.), *The Cambridge Companion to Dante* (Cambridge University Press, 1993).

A Note on the Translation

'Nothing that has been harmoniously composed in poetic form can be translated from its own language to another without destroying its sweetness and harmony.'[1] These words of Dante's have abashed many translators but deterred few. Of course one cannot adequately reproduce the sweetness and harmony of Dante's poems but one owes it to him at least to attempt to approach it in rhyme. Dante loved rhyme: *concatenatio pulcra* ('beautiful linkage'), he called it, and took pleasure in the closure of a couplet which 'with rhyme falls into silence'.[2] It is usually said, and I said so myself in my note to the first edition of this translation, that English has fewer rhymes than Italian. I wish now to recant my words. Since then I have translated Ariosto's *Orlando Furioso* into rhymed octaves and have discovered the many resources of English, which, owing to our abundance of diphthongs, is in fact more plentiful in rhymes than Italian.

I have aimed at lucidity as well as strictness of form and can only hope that, despite Dante's misgivings, something of sweetness and harmony has been achieved.

NOTES

1. *Il Convivio*, Book I, chapter 7.
2. *De Vulgari Eloquentia*, Book II, chapter 13.

LA VITA NUOVA

I

In the book of my memory, after the first pages, which are almost blank, there is a section headed *Incipit vita nova*.[1] Beneath this heading I find the words which it is my intention to copy into this smaller book, or if not all, at least their meaning.

II

Nine times the heaven of the light had revolved in its own movement since my birth and had almost returned to the same point when the woman whom my mind beholds in glory first appeared before my eyes. She was called Beatrice by many who did not know what it meant to call her this. She had lived in this world for the length of time in which the heaven of the fixed stars had circled one twelfth of a degree towards the East. Thus she had not long passed the beginning of her ninth year when she appeared to me and I was almost at the end of mine when I beheld her. She was dressed in a very noble colour, a decorous and delicate crimson, tied with a girdle and trimmed in a manner suited to her tender age. The moment I saw her I say in all truth that the vital spirit, which dwells in the inmost depths of the heart, began to tremble so violently that I felt the vibration alarmingly in all my pulses, even the weakest of them. As it trembled, it uttered these words: *Ecce deus fortior me, qui*

---

1.   Here begins the period of my boyhood. (See Introduction.)

veniens dominabitur mihi.[1] At this point, the spirit of the senses which dwells on high in the place to which all our sense perceptions are carried, was filled with amazement and, speaking especially to the spirits of vision, made this pronouncement: *Apparuit iam beatitudo vestra.*[2] Whereupon the natural spirit, which dwells where our nourishment is digested, began to weep and, weeping, said: *Heu miser! quia frequenter impeditus ero deinceps.*[3] From then on indeed Love ruled over my soul, which was thus wedded to him early in life, and he began to acquire such assurance and mastery over me, owing to the power which my imagination gave him, that I was obliged to fulfil all his wishes perfectly. He often commanded me to go where perhaps I might see this angelic child and so, while I was still a boy, I often went in search of her; and I saw that in all her ways she was so praiseworthy and noble that indeed the words of the poet Homer might have been said of her: 'She did not seem the daughter of a mortal man, but of a god.' Though her image, which was always present in my mind, incited Love to dominate me, its influence was so noble that it never allowed Love to guide me without the faithful counsel of reason, in everything in which such counsel was useful to hear. But, since to dwell on the feelings and actions of such early years might appear to some to be fictitious, I will move on and, omitting many things which might be copied from the mastertext from which the foregoing is derived, I come now to words inscribed in my memory under more important headings.

III

When exactly nine years had passed since this gracious being appeared to me, as I have described, it happened that on the last day of this intervening period this marvel appeared before me

1. Behold a god more powerful than I who comes to rule over me (i.e. Love).
2. Now your source of joy has been revealed.
3. Woe is me! for I shall often be impeded from now on.

again, dressed in purest white, walking between two other women of distinguished bearing, both older than herself. As they walked down the street she turned her eyes towards me where I stood in fear and trembling, and with her ineffable courtesy, which is now rewarded in eternal life, she greeted me; and such was the virtue of her greeting that I seemed to experience the height of bliss. It was exactly the ninth hour of day when she gave me her sweet greeting. As this was the first time she had ever spoken to me, I was filled with such joy that, my senses reeling, I had to withdraw from the sight of others. So I returned to the loneliness of my room and began to think about this gracious person. As I thought of her I fell asleep and a marvellous vision appeared to me. In my room I seemed to see a cloud the colour of fire, and in the cloud a lordly figure, frightening to behold, yet in himself, it seemed to me, he was filled with a marvellous joy. He said many things, of which I understood only a few; among them were the words: *Ego dominus tuus.*[1] In his arms I seemed to see a naked figure, sleeping, wrapped lightly in a crimson cloth. Gazing intently I saw it was she who had bestowed her greeting on me earlier that day. In one hand the standing figure held a fiery object, and he seemed to say, *Vide cor tuum.*[2] After a little while I thought he wakened her who slept and prevailed on her to eat the glowing object in his hand. Reluctantly and hesitantly she did so. A few moments later his happiness turned to bitter grief, and, weeping, he gathered the figure in his arms and together they seemed to ascend into the heavens. I felt such anguish at their departure that my light sleep was broken, and I awoke. On reflecting, I realized at once that the vision had appeared to me in the fourth hour of the night, that is, the first of the last nine hours of the night. Pondering what I had seen in my dream, I decided to make it known to a number of poets who were famous at that time. As I had already tried my hand at the art of composing in rhyme, I decided to write a sonnet in which I would greet all Love's faithful servants; and so, requesting them to interpret my dream,

1. I am your Master.
2. Behold your heart.

I described what I had seen in my sleep. This was the sonnet
40 beginning: *To every captive soul . . .*

> To every captive soul and gentle lover
>   Into whose sight this present rhyme may chance,
>   That, writing back, each may expound its sense,
>   Greetings in Love, who is their Lord, I offer.
> Already of those hours a third was over
>   Wherein all stars display their radiance,
>   When lo! Love stood before me in my trance:
>   Recalling what he was fills me with horror.
> Joyful Love seemed to me and in his keeping
>   He held my heart; and in his arms there lay
>   My lady in a mantle wrapped, and sleeping.
>   Then he awoke her and, her fear not heeding,
>   My burning heart fed to her reverently.
>   Then he departed from my vision, weeping.

This sonnet is divided into two parts. In the first I extend a
greeting and ask for a reply; in the second I convey what it is
that requires a reply. The second part begins: *Already of those
hours . . .*

45   This sonnet drew replies from many, who all had different
opinions as to its meaning. Among those who replied was some-
one whom I call my closest friend; he wrote a sonnet beginning:
In my opinion you beheld all virtue.

        Our friendship dated from the time he learned that it was I
50 who had sent him the sonnet. The true meaning of the dream
was not then perceived by anyone, but now it is perfectly clear
to the simplest reader.

IV

1   From that vision onwards my natural spirit began to be impeded
in its functioning, for my soul was wholly given to thoughts of
this most gracious person. In a short time I grew so frail and

weak that many of my friends felt concern at my appearance.
Many others, full of malicious curiosity, were doing their best
to discover things about me which I particularly wished to con-
ceal; and, perceiving the mischievous intent of their inquiries, in
obedience to Love's will, who commanded me in accordance
with the counsel of reason, I replied that it was Love who had
reduced me to this state. I said this because I bore so many of
Love's signs in my face that they could not be hidden. And when
they asked me: 'For whom has Love thus dealt with you?', I
looked at them with a smile and said nothing.

V

One day it happened that this most gracious lady was sitting in
a place where words about the Queen of glory were heard, and
I was in a position from which I could behold my joy; and
between us, in direct line with my vision, there sat another
lady of very pleasing appearance who looked at me repeatedly,
astonished by my gaze, which seemed directed at her. A number
of people observed this and soon began to draw conclusions, so
much so that as I was leaving I heard someone behind me say:
'Look how he pines for love of her', and at the mention of her
name I understood that he was referring to the lady who had
sat in the direct line between the most gracious Beatrice and my
gaze. Then I was greatly reassured, feeling confident that my
gaze had not revealed my secret to anyone that day. It was then
I hit on the idea of making this lady a screen to hide the truth;
and I pretended so well that in a short time most of those who
talked about me believed they knew my secret. This lady was
my screen for several years and months, and to make it the more
convincing I wrote a few little things for her in rhyme which I
do not intend to include unless they relate to the theme of that
most gracious lady, Beatrice. This being so, I will omit them all
apart from one which can be seen to be in praise of her.

VI

1   During the time when this lady served as the screen of so great
a love on my part, there came to me the desire to record the
name of her who was of all women the most gracious, and to
accompany it with the names of many other women, in particu-
5   lar the name of my gentle screen-lady. And so I made a list of
the sixty most beautiful women in the city where the Almighty
willed that my lady should live, and I composed an epistle in the
form of a *serventese*, which I shall not include. I would not
have mentioned it except to relate the wonderful thing which
10   occurred when I composed it, that is, that the name of my lady
would not fit anywhere but ninth in order among the names of
all the others.

VII

1   The lady who for so long had screened my true feelings was
obliged to leave the city I have mentioned and go to a distant
town. Dismayed by the loss of my beautiful defence, I was
greatly cast down, more than I would have thought possible.
5   Thinking that if I did not write sorrowfully on the theme of her
departure people would soon become aware of my pretence, I
decided to compose a lament in the form of a sonnet. This I will
transcribe because my lady was the immediate cause of certain
words which it includes, as is plain to anyone who understands
10   it. And so I wrote this sonnet which begins: *O you who on the
road of Love pass by* . . .

> O you who on the road of Love pass by,
>   Attend and see
>   If any grief there be as heavy as mine.
>   Hear me and then consider: am not I
>   The keep and key
>   Of all the torments sorrow can combine?

> Not my slight worth but Love's nobility
> Did once to me
> A life of sweet serenity assign.
> Often behind me I would hear men sigh:
> 'How can he be
> 'Deserving of such joy beyond confine?'
> All my elation now has ebbed away
> Which once came flowing from Love's treasure-store,
> And I, now poor,
> Lack even words, and know not what to say.
> And so, like those who secretly endure,
> Their needs concealing from the light of day,
> In aspect gay,
> Within my heart I pine and grieve the more.

This sonnet has two principal parts. In the first my intention is to call on the faithful followers of Love in the words of the prophet Jeremiah: *O vos omnes qui transitis per viam, attendite et videte si est dolor sicut meus*,[1] and to entreat them to hear me. In the second part I tell where Love had placed me, with a meaning other than the one conveyed by the beginning and end of the sonnet, and I tell what I have lost. The second part begins: *Not my slight worth . . .*

VIII

After the departure of this lady, it pleased the Lord of the angels to call to His glory a young woman of gentle bearing who had graced the city with her loveliness. I saw her lifeless body lying where many women were mourning piteously over it. When I remembered that I had seen her formerly in the company of my most gracious one I could not help shedding a few tears. As I wept I decided to compose something about her death, in tribute

---

1. All ye that pass by, behold and see if there be any sorrow like unto my sorrow. (*The Lamentations of Jeremiah*, i, 12.)

to the fact that I had seen her one time with my lady. I touched
on this in the last part of the words which I composed about
10 her, as is plain to anyone who understands. So I wrote these two
sonnets; the first begins: *Love weeps . . .* ; and the second: *Death
villainous and cruel . . .*

> Love weeps; so, lovers, come and weep likewise,
>   And stay to learn the reason for his tears.
>   Ladies lamenting piteously Love hears,
>   Shedding a bitter sorrow from their eyes,
>   For in a heart whose nature gentle is
>   The cruel handiwork of Death appears.
>   All that the world, save honour, most reveres
>   In gracious womanhood in ruin lies.
> How Love has honoured her now let me say:
>   In his true form I saw him mourning there
>   Beside her lifeless image, full of grace.
>   Often he raised his eyes toward the place
>   Where straightway sped the noble soul of her
>   Who was a woman once so fair and gay.

This first sonnet is divided into three parts. In the first I address
the faithful servants of Love, calling on them to weep, for their
15 Lord is weeping. I say, 'Stay to learn the reason for his tears', to
induce them to listen to me. In the second part I relate the cause;
in the third I tell of the honour which Love paid this lady. The
second part begins: *Ladies lamenting . . .* ; the third part begins:
How Love has honoured her . . .

> Death villainous and cruel, pity's foe,
>   Thou ancient womb of woe,
>   Burden of judgement irreversible!
>   Since thou my heart with cause of grief dost fill,
>   Whence with sad thoughts I dwell,
>   Reviling thee my tongue must weary grow.
>   If in the eyes of men I'd bring thee low,
>   I shall be forced to show
>   The evil wrongs of which thou'rt culpable.

    Not that such felony is new to tell,
    But thus the wrath to swell
    In any who to Love for nurture go.
The world thou hast despoiled of courtesy
    And all of women's virtue that men praise.
    Of her gay, youthful days
    The loveliness thou hast slain wantonly.
    No more will I disclose who she may be,
    Except by naming her known qualities.
    Who does not merit grace
    Let him ne'er hope to have her company.

This sonnet is divided into four parts. In the first I call Death by
some of its true names; in the second, still addressing Death, I
give the reason why I am moved to revile it; in the third, I
vituperate it; in the fourth I turn to address a person left unde-
fined, although defined in my own intention. The second part
begins: *Since thou my heart . . .* ; the third begins: *If in the
eyes . . .* ; the fourth begins: *Who does not merit . . .*

IX

A few days after the death of this lady, an event occurred which
made it necessary for me to leave the city I have mentioned, and
travel in the direction of the region where the lady who had
been my screen was now living, though my destination did not
take me quite so far. I was in the company of a great many
people, outwardly at least, but I found the journey so irksome
that my sighs could barely relieve the anguish I felt in my
heart on drawing farther and farther away from my source of
happiness. And that sweetest Lord who held sway over me by
virtue of my most gracious lady appeared in my imagination
like a traveller, dressed in simple, humble clothing. He seemed
dejected and kept his gaze on the ground, except that from time
to time he turned his eyes towards a beautiful stream of clearest
water which flowed beside the road on which I journeyed. Love

15 seemed to call my name and say: 'I have come from the lady
who for a long time has been your defence; I know now that her
return will be long deferred and so I have brought back the heart
which you gave her at my command. I am taking it to another
who will be your new defence (and as he named her I realized
20 that I knew her well). Be careful if you repeat any of what I have
told you to do so in such a way that no one perceives the
simulated nature of the love which you have shown this lady
and which you must now show to another.' When he had said
this he vanished suddenly, as though merging a great part of
25 himself with me; and somewhat altered in my appearance, I
rode on that day very pensive, sighing a great deal. Later, from
these events, I began to compose this sonnet, which begins: *As
I rode forth one day . . .*

> As I rode forth one day not long ago,
>> Pensive about my journey and distressed,
>> I met Love, like a traveller, humbly dressed,
>> Coming along my path, forlorn and slow.
>> Such wretchedness his aspect seemed to show,
>> He might have been a monarch dispossessed.
>> With thoughtful steps and sighing he progressed,
>> His gaze averted and his head held low.
> When he caught sight of me he called my name
>> And said: 'From far away I bring your heart,
>> Where it has dwelt, according to my will,
>> And take it a new service to fulfil.'
>> Then I absorbed of him so great a part,
>> He vanished just as strangely as he came.

This sonnet has three parts. In the first I relate how I met Love
30 and how he looked; in the second I tell what he said to me,
though not everything for fear of revealing my secret; in the
third I tell how he disappeared. The second part begins: *When
he caught sight of me . . .* ; the third begins: *Then I absorbed . . .*

X

When I returned I went in search of the lady whom Love had   1
mentioned to me on the road of sighs. To speak briefly, in a
short time I made her my defence, but to such an extent that too
many people talked about it beyond the bounds of courtesy.
This often weighed heavily on me. For this reason, that is to say,   5
because of excessive rumours which, it seems, were maliciously
defaming me, that most gracious being, the queen of virtue, in
whose presence all evil was destroyed, one day as she passed by
refused me her sweetest greeting, in which resided all my joy.
And now, departing somewhat from the immediate subject, I   10
want to explain the miraculous effect of her greeting upon me.

XI

Whenever and wherever she appeared, in the hope of receiving   1
her miraculous salutation I felt I had not an enemy in the world.
Indeed, I glowed with a flame of charity which moved me to
forgive all who had ever injured me; and if at that moment
someone had asked me a question, about anything, my only   5
reply would have been: 'Love', with a countenance clothed with
humility. When she was on the point of bestowing her greeting,
a spirit of love, destroying all the other spirits of the senses,
drove away the frail spirits of vision and said: 'Go and pay
homage to your lady'; and Love himself remained in their place.   10
Anyone wanting to behold Love could have done so then by
watching the quivering of my eyes. And when this most gracious
being actually bestowed the saving power of her salutation, I do
not say that Love as an intermediary could dim for me such
unendurable bliss but, almost by excess of sweetness, his influ-   15
ence was such that my body, which was then utterly given over
to his governance, often moved like a heavy, inanimate object.
So it is plain that in her greeting resided all my joy, which often
exceeded and overflowed my capacity.

XII

1   Now, returning to my subject, I say that after such bliss had
been withheld from me I was so overwhelmed with grief that,
shunning all company, I went to a solitary place where I
drenched the earth with bitter tears. When this weeping had
5   eased a little, I shut myself in my room where I could continue
my lament without being heard. And there, asking pity of the
Lady of courtesy and crying, 'Love, help your faithful one', I
fell asleep in the midst of my weeping, like a little child that has
been beaten. About half-way through my sleep I seemed to see
10 beside me in my room a young man dressed in whitest garments;
from his bearing he seemed to be thinking deeply, gazing at me
where I lay. After looking at me for some time, he sighed and
called me by my name; then he said these words to me: *Fili mi,
tempus est ut praetermictantur simulacra nostra.*[1] Then I seemed
15 to recognize him because he called me in the way he had often
called me in my sleep. As I looked at him again I saw him
weeping piteously and he seemed to be waiting for me to say
something; so, taking courage, I began to talk with him as
follows: 'Lord of nobility of soul, why do you weep?' And he
20 replied: *Ego tanquam centrum circuli, cui simili modo se habent
circumferentiae partes; tu autem non sic.*[2] As I pondered his
words, it seemed to me that he had spoken in a very obscure
manner, so I forced myself to ask: 'Lord, what is it that you are
saying to me so obscurely?' And he replied in the vernacular:
25 'Do not ask more than is useful for you!' Then I began to talk
with him about the greeting which had been denied me and I
asked him the reason. He replied as follows: 'Our Lady Beatrice
was informed by certain people who were discussing you that
the lady whom I mentioned to you on the road of sighs had met
30 with some discourtesy from you; and so, this most gracious
being, who is the contrary of all that is discourteous, did not

1.   My son, it is time for our false images to be put aside.
2.   I am like the centre of a circle, to which the parts of the circumference are
related in similar manner; you, however, are not.

deign to greet you, fearing you might be importunate. Therefore, since your long-kept secret is in truth already partly known to her, I want you to compose something in rhyme in which you will tell of the power I have over you on her account, and how you were hers straightway, ever since your boyhood. And as witness of that, call on him who knows it and say how you entreat him to tell her; and I, who am he, will gladly prove it to her. In this way she will come to know your true desire and will see how mistaken are the words of those who speak wrongly about you. Make your verses a kind of intermediary, for it is not fitting to address her directly; and do not send them anywhere where she might hear them without sending me with them; adorn them with a sweet harmony, in which I shall be present whenever I am required.' When he had said this he vanished and my sleep was broken. Reflecting on it, I discovered that this vision had occurred at the ninth hour of the day; and before I left my room I decided to compose a ballad in which I would fulfil my Lord's commands. Later I did write it and it begins: *My Ballad, I would have you seek* . . .

> My Ballad, I would have you seek out Love
>   And to the presence of my Lady bring,
>   That the excuses which for me you sing
>   He may by reasoned argument improve.
>
> So courteous, my Ballad, are your ways,
>   That unaccompanied
>   You well might venture anywhere;
>   But if in safety you would pass with ease
>   Seek out Love first, I bid.
>   Unwise it were to go without him there,
>   For she to whom these messages you bear,
>   As I believe, with me is so aggrieved
>   That in his absence being ill-received
>   You'd meet with coldness and the shame thereof.

Entering with Love – an embassy of two –
  Begin, with music sweet,
  (When you have pleaded for her clemency):
  'My Lady, he who bade me come to you
  This favour does entreat:
  If an excuse he has, hear it from me.
  Using your beauty, Love – whom here you see –
  Can make him, as he wills, change countenance.
  If at another, then, Love made him glance,
  His heart being constant, think not to reprove.

  'Lady, his heart has ever been steadfast
  In homage so devout,
  In all his thoughts to serve you he pays heed,
  Unwaveringly yours, from first to last.'
  If she remain in doubt
  Let her ask Love who knows the truth indeed.
  Then lastly for this favour humbly plead:
  If to grant pardon should her patience try
  Let her send word commanding me to die;
  Not disobedient will her servant prove.

And then with Love, compassion's key, confer
  (Before your leave you take)
  For he will plead my cause to her with skill:
  'By means of my sweet music stay with her
  And for your servant's sake
  Concerning him hold converse as you will.
  If your request for pardon she fulfil
  By her fair smile may she forgiveness show.'
  My gentle Ballad, when you please to go
  At a propitious moment make your move.

This ballad is divided into three parts. In the first I tell it where
to go and bid it to go safely, telling it what company to take if
it wants to avoid all danger; in the second I say what it must
convey; in the third I set it free to go when it will, commending
55 it on its departure to the arms of fortune. The second part

begins: *Entering with Love* . . . ; the third begins: *My gentle Ballad* . . .

Someone might object that it is not clear to whom I address my words in the second person, since the ballad is nothing other than the words I write; and so I say that I intend to clarify and resolve this doubt later on in this little book, with reference to a still more doubtful passage. Then if anyone has a doubt or wishes to raise an objection about this part, let him defer it till later, when he will understand.

XIII

After the vision which I have described, when I had composed the rhymes which Love had commanded me, a number of conflicting thoughts began to contend and strive one with the other, all of them, it seemed, unanswerably. Among them were four which seemed most to disturb my peace of mind. One was this: 'The domination of Love is a good thing because he guides the mind of his faithful follower away from all unworthiness.' Another thought was this: 'The domination of Love is not good because the more faithfully a follower serves him, the more burdensome and grievous are the moments he must endure'; yet another thought was as follows: 'The name of Love is so sweet to hear that it seems impossible that it can be anything but sweet in its effect upon most things, for it is known that names are a consequence of the things which are named, as it is written, *Nomina sunt consequentia rerum*';[1] the fourth thought was this: 'The Lady for whom Love holds you so enthralled is not like other women whose hearts are easily moved.' Every one of these thoughts so contended within me that I became like a person who does not know which road to take on his journey, who wants to set out but does not know where to start. The only way I could see of reconciling them all was one which was very distasteful to me; that is, to call on Pity and throw myself into

1.   Names are the consequences of things.

her arms. And as I lingered in this state, I felt a desire to compose
something about it in rhyme; and so I wrote this sonnet, which
25 begins: *All thoughts within my mind* . . .

> All thoughts within my mind discourse of Love
>   And have among them great diversity:
>   One makes me long for Love's authority,
>   Another its unreason seeks to prove,
>   Then sweetness, as of hope, I'm conscious of.
>   Another makes me weep incessantly.
>   Only in asking pity all agree,
>   Trembling in fear with which the pulses throb.
> And so I know not from which theme to start;
>   And I would write, yet know not what to say.
>   Thus in a maze of Love I'm wandering!
>   And if to harmony all these I'd bring
>   My enemy I must bring into play,
>   My lady Pity, to defend my part.

This sonnet can be divided into four parts. In the first I imagine
that all my thoughts are of Love; in the second I say that they
are all different and I describe their diversity; in the third I say
what they all appear to have in common; in the fourth I say that
30 wishing to write about Love I do not know which thought to
take as my theme; and if I want to combine them all I am obliged
to call on my enemy, my lady Pity; and I say 'my lady' as a
scornful way of speaking. The second part begins: *And have
among them* . . . ; the third: *Only in asking pity* . . . ; and the
35 fourth: *And so I know not* . . .

XIV

1 After the battle of conflicting thoughts it happened that this
most gracious person was present where many women were
gathered together. I too was taken there by a friend who thought
it would give me great pleasure to be present where so many

beautiful women were to be seen. Hardly knowing where I was   5
being taken, and trusting the person who in fact had brought
his friend almost to the verge of death, I said: 'Why have we
come to visit these ladies?' And he replied: 'To wait on them in
a manner that is fitting.' The truth is that they were gathered
there in the company of a lady who had been married that day   10
and, according to the custom of that city, it was their duty to
keep her company on the first occasion when she sat down at
table in the house of her bridegroom. Thinking that it would
please my friend, I consented to stay and attend on the ladies
who were present. Just as I had reached this decision, I felt the 15
beginning of an extraordinary throbbing on the left side of my
breast which immediately spread to all the parts of my body.
Then, pretending nothing was wrong, I leaned for support
against a fresco painted in a frieze round the walls of the house.
Afraid that other people might notice how I was trembling, I   20
raised my eyes and as they rested on the women gathered there
I saw among them the most gracious Beatrice. Then my spirits
were so routed by the power which Love acquired on finding
himself so close to this most gracious being that none survived
except the spirits of vision; and even they were driven from their 25
organs because Love himself desired to occupy their noble
place in order to behold her who inspired such wonder.
Although I was anything but myself, I was very much grieved
for these little spirits who lamented loudly, saying: 'If this Lord
had not flung us from our rightful place like a bolt of lightning, 30
we could have stayed to behold the marvel of this lady, as
all our fellows are doing!' A number of the women present,
observing my transformation, began to be astonished and, talk-
ing about it, they mocked at me in company with the most
gracious one herself. Then my friend who, in all good faith, had 35
been so mistaken as to bring me there, took me by the hand,
and, removing me from the sight of the women, asked what was
troubling me. Then, when I had rested a little and my lifeless
spirits had revived, and those which had been expelled had
returned to their rightful estate, I said to my friend: 'I had set 40
foot in that part of life beyond which one cannot go with any
hope of returning.' Then I left him and returned to my room of

tears, where, weeping and suffering the agony of shame, I said
to myself: 'If my lady knew of my condition, I do not believe
45   she would so mock at my appearance; indeed, I think she would
feel great compassion.' And while I was still weeping I decided
to compose verses addressed to her, explaining the reason for
my change of countenance, saying that I was aware that people
did not know of it and that if it were known it would arouse
50   compassion. I decided to do this, hoping that the verses might
perchance be heard by her; so later I wrote this sonnet, which
begins: *With your companions . . .*

> With your companions you make fun of me,
>   Not thinking, Lady, what the reason is
>   I cut so strange a figure in your eyes
> When, raising mine, your loveliness I see.
> If you but knew, Pity no more could be
> Severe towards me in her usual guise.
> Finding me near you, Love his weapons tries.
> Gaining in boldness and temerity,
> And on my frightened spirits rains such blows
>   That some he slays and others flee in fear,
>   Till only he is left to look on you.
> Hence I am altered into someone new,
>   Yet not so that I do not plainly hear
>   My outcast spirits wailing in their woes.

I will not subdivide this sonnet as such analysis is made only in
order to disclose the meaning. Therefore, since from the account
55   I have given of its occasion this sonnet is quite clear, there is no
need to divide it. I admit that among the words in which I set
forth the occasion of the sonnet there are some whose meaning
is obscure, for instance, when I say that Love slays all my spirits,
except the spirits of vision, which survive but are driven forth
60   from their organs. It is impossible to explain this to anyone who
is not to the same extent a faithful follower of Love; and to
those who are it is obvious what the meaning is. Consequently
there is no point in my clarifying that doubt because such
clarification would be either useless or superfluous.

XV

After this strange transformation, an insistent thought came to me and would hardly ever leave me. It repeatedly took possession of me, reasoning as follows: 'Since you take on such an absurd appearance whenever you are near this lady, why do you still try to see her? Suppose she asked you this, what would you reply, assuming that all your faculties were unimpeded and you were able to reply?' To this another, humble, thought made answer: 'If I did not lose my wits and were confident enough to reply to her, I would tell her that as soon as I imagine her wonderful beauty the desire to see her takes possession of me, and this desire is so powerful that it utterly destroys anything in my memory that might rise up against it; that is why my past sufferings do not restrain me from trying to see her.' And so, stirred by such thoughts, I decided to write something to excuse myself to her in relation to this insistent thought, and at the same time explaining what happens to me when I am near her. And I wrote this sonnet which begins: *All thoughts of what befalls me . . .*

> All thoughts of what befalls me die away,
>   Fair jewel, when to see you I draw nigh;
>   When I am close to you I hear Love say:
>   'If you fear Death, now is the time to fly!'
>   My looks the colour of my heart betray
>   Which, fainting, for support leans all awry;
>   And in this tremor as I reel and sway
>   The very stones I walk on echo 'Die!'
> A sin do those commit who see me then
>   And do not comfort me in my soul's plight,
>   At least by showing that they grieve for me,
>   For Pity's sake which, by your mocking slain,
>   Is brought to life anew in the dead sight
>   Of eyes which have no more desire to see.

This sonnet is divided into two parts. In the first I give the reason
why I do not stop myself from seeking this lady's company; in
the second I describe what happens to me when I draw near her.
This second part begins: *When I am close to you* . . . This
also can be subdivided into five sections, according to the five
different things which are narrated. In the first of these I say
what Love, advised by reason, says to me when I am near her;
in the second I convey the condition of my heart as it is shown
in my face; in the third I relate how I lose all confidence; in the
fourth I say that anyone who does not show compassion for me
is guilty of sin, for to do so would give me some comfort; and
in the last I say why people should have compassion, that is,
because of the piteous look which comes into my eyes. This
piteousness is slain, that is, rendered imperceptible, by my lady's
mockery, which leads others who perhaps might notice this
piteousness to do as she does. The second subdivision begins:
My looks the colour . . . ; the third: *And in this tremor* . . . ; the
fourth: *A sin do those commit* . . . ; and the fifth: *For Pity's
sake* . . .

XVI

When I had finished this sonnet I felt the desire to write another
in which I would say four more things about my state which it
seemed to me I had not yet made plain. The first was that I
was often distressed when memory stirred my imagination to
consider the effect which Love was having on me; the second
was that frequently Love assailed me so violently that nothing
remained alive in me except a thought which spoke of my lady;
the third was that when the battle of Love raged within me in
this way, I felt impelled, all pale as I was, to go and see my lady,
believing that the sight of her would give me protection from
this battle, quite forgetting what happened to me when I drew
near such graciousness; the fourth relates how the sight of her
not only did not offer me protection but finally defeated what

little life I had left. That was how I came to write the sonnet
which begins: *Many a time the thought* . . .   15

> Many a time the thought returns to me:
>   What sad conditions Love on me bestows!
>   And moved by Pity I say frequently:
>   'Can there be anyone who my state knows?'
>   For Love takes hold of me so suddenly
>   My vital spirits I am near to lose.
>   One only of them all survives in me,
>   And to its words of you its life it owes.
> To aid me then my forces I renew,
>   And pallid, all my courage drained long since,
>   I come to you to remedy my plight;
>   But if I raise my eyes to look at you
>   So vast a tremor in my heart begins
>   My beating pulses put my soul to flight.

This sonnet is divided into four parts, related to the four matters
which it narrates and, because they are explained above, I will
confine myself to indicating the parts by their beginnings, as
follows: the second part begins: *For Love takes hold* . . . ; the
third: *To aid me then* . . . ; and the fourth: *But if I raise* . . .   20

XVII

When I had written these three sonnets, which are addressed   1
directly to my lady, I had said almost everything about my state
and I thought it right to be silent and say no more, for I felt I had
explained enough about myself. Although from then onwards I
refrained from writing verses addressed to her, I felt impelled to   5
take up a new and nobler theme than before. As the occasion of
finding my new theme is agreeable to hear, I will narrate it, as
briefly as I can.

XVIII

1   As many people had guessed from my appearance the secret of
     my heart, a certain group of ladies, who were aware of my
     feelings, having witnessed my discomfiture at one time or
     another, had gathered together to enjoy each other's company.
5   As I passed by, led as though by fortune, one of them called me.
     She had so delightful a way of speaking that when I had drawn
     close to them and had made quite sure that my lady was not
     among them, I took courage and greeted them, asking them
     how I could be of service to them. There were many ladies
10   present, some laughing together, others looking at me, waiting
     to hear what I would say, and still others talking among them-
     selves. One of these, turning her eyes towards me and addressing
     me by name, said: 'What is the point of your love for your lady
     since you are unable to endure her presence? Tell us, for surely
15   the aim of such love must be unique!' When she had finished
     speaking not only she, but all the others seemed from their
     appearance to be waiting for my answer. Then I said to them:
     'Ladies, the aim of my love was once the greeting of one of
     whom perhaps you are aware, and in that resided all my blessed-
20   ness and joy, for it was the aim and end of all my desires; but
     ever since she saw fit to deny me her greeting, my lord Love, in
     his mercy, has placed all my hope of that same joy in something
     which cannot fail me.' At this they began to talk among them-
     selves, and just as sometimes we see rain falling mingled with
25   beautiful flakes of snow, so it seemed to me their words mingled
     with their sighs. When they had conversed together for a while,
     she who had first addressed me said: 'We ask you to tell us in
     what this joy of yours resides!' And I, in reply to her, said this:
     'In words which praise my lady.' She answered: 'If you were
30   telling the truth, those words you have composed to describe
     your state would have been written in such a way as to convey
     a different meaning.' Thinking this over, I moved away feeling
     almost ashamed, saying to myself: 'Since there is so much joy in
     words which praise my lady, why have I ever written in any

other manner?' And so I decided to take as the theme of my   35
writing from then on whatever was praise of this most gracious
being. Reflecting deeply on this, it seemed to me that I had
undertaken too lofty a theme for my powers, so much so that I
was afraid to enter upon it; and so I remained for several days
desiring to write and afraid to begin.   40

XIX

Then it happened that as I was walking along a path beside   1
which flowed a stream of very clear water so strong an urge to
write came over me that I began to think how I should set about
it. I thought it would not be fitting to speak of my lady to anyone
except other women, whom I should address in the second   5
person, and not to any woman but only to those who are
gracious, not merely feminine. Then my tongue spoke, almost
as though moved of its own accord, and said: 'Ladies who know
by insight what love is.' With great joy I stored these words
away in my mind, intending to use them as an opening for my   10
rhyme. Then when I had returned to the city, I pondered for
several days and finally I began a *canzone* which opens with
these words, and is composed in a manner which will appear
evident when I come to divide it. The *canzone* begins: *Ladies
who know . . .*   15

> Ladies who know by insight what love is,
>> With you about my Lady I would treat,
>> Not that I think her praises I'll complete,
>> But seeking by my words to ease my mind.
> When I consider all her qualities
> I say that Love steals over me so sweet
> That if my courage then did not retreat
> By speaking I'd enamour all mankind.
> Yet words not too exalted I would find,
> Lest base timidity my mind possess;

But lightly touch upon her graciousness,
Leaving her worth by this to be divined,
With you, ladies and maidens who know love.
To others it may not be spoken of.

To the all-knowing mind an angel prays:
  'Lord, in the world a miracle proceeds,
  In act and visible, from a soul's deeds,
  Whose splendour reaches to this very height.'
One imperfection only Heaven has:
  The lack of her; so now for her it pleads
  And every saint with clamour intercedes.
  Only compassion is our advocate.
God understands to whom their prayers relate
  And answers them: 'My loved ones, bear in peace
  That she, your hope, remain until I please
  Where one knows he must lose her, soon or late,
  And who will say in Hell: "Souls unconfessed!
  I have beheld the hope of Heaven's blessed."'

My lady is desired in highest heaven.
  Now of her excellence I'd have you hear.
  All ladies who would noble be, draw near
  And walk with her, for as she goes her way
A chill in evil hearts by Love is driven,
  Causing all thoughts to freeze and perish there.
  If any such endured to look on her
  He would be changed to good or die straightway.
If any man she find who worthy be
  To look at her, her virtue then he knows,
  For, greeting him, salvation she bestows,
  In meekness melting every grudge away.
With further grace has God endowed her still:
  Whoe'er did speak with her shall not fare ill.

Love says of her: 'How can a mortal thing
  Have purity and beauty such as hers?'
  Then looks again and to himself he swears

A marvel she must be which God intends.
Pearl-like, not to excess, her colouring,
As suited to a lady's face, appears.
She is the sum of nature's universe.
To her perfection all of beauty tends.
Forth from her eyes, where'er her gaze she bends,
Come spirits flaming with the power of love.
Whoever sees her then, his eyes they prove,
Passing within until the heart each finds.
You will see Love depicted in her smile,
Where none may gaze save for a little while.

My song, you will go parleying, I know,
With many ladies, when I give consent.
Since I have raised you without ornament
As Love's young daughter, hear now what I say.
Of those about you, beg assistance, so:
'Tell me which way to take, for I am sent
To her whose praise is my embellishment.'
If you would journey there without delay
Among the base and vulgar do not stay.
Contrive to show your meaning, if you can,
Only to ladies or a courteous man.
They will conduct you by the quickest way.
You will find Love abiding with her beauty.
Commend me to my Lord, as is your duty.

So that this *canzone* may be well understood, I will divide it
more minutely than the previous verses. First of all I divide it
into three main parts; the first is a prelude to the words which
follow; the second is the subject with which I deal; the third is
like an attendant on the words which precede it. The second 20
begins: *To the all-knowing mind* . . . ; and the third: *My song,
you will go parleying* . . . The first part is subdivided into four
sections. In the first I state to whom I wish to speak concerning
my lady and why I wish to speak of her; in the second I describe
the condition in which I find myself when I think of her virtue 25
and what I would say if I did not lose courage; in the third I say

how I think I must speak of her in order not to be hindered by misgivings; in the fourth, restating to whom I wish to speak, I give the reason why. The second of these sections begins: *When I consider . . .* ; the third: *Yet words not too exalted . . .* and the fourth: *With you, ladies . . .*

Next, where I say: *To the all-knowing mind . . .* I begin to treat of my lady and this part is divided into two sections. In the first I say what the thoughts of Heaven are concerning her; in the second I say what is thought of her on earth, beginning: *My lady is desired . . .* This second section is further subdivided into two; first I speak of the nobility of her soul and relate some of the effective powers which emanate from it; secondly I speak of the nobility of her person, mentioning some of her beauties, beginning: *Love says of her . . .* This second section is also further subdivided into two, for I speak first of the beauties of her whole person, and secondly of the beauty of certain parts of her person, beginning: *Forth from her eyes . . .* Here again this subsection is divided into yet another two parts; in the first I speak of her eyes, which are the beginning of love; in the second I speak of her mouth, which is the end and aim of love. And to eliminate here and now all evil thought, let the reader remember what is written above about my lady's salutation, which was an operation of her mouth, and was the object of all my desires for as long as it was granted to me.

Finally, where I say: *My song, you will go parleying . . .* I add a stanza to serve almost as a handmaiden to the others, in which I say what I desire of my *canzone*. As this last part is simple to understand I will not involve myself in further divisions. Certainly to uncover still more meaning in this *canzone* it would be necessary to divide it more minutely; but if anyone has not the wit to understand it with the help of the divisions already made he had best leave it alone. Indeed I am afraid that I may have conveyed its meaning to too many by dividing it even as I have done, if it should come to the ears of too many.

new definition of love

XX

When this *canzone* had circulated among a number of people,   1
a friend who heard it was moved to ask me to write saying what
Love is, having perhaps, because of the verses he had heard,
greater confidence in me than I deserved. So, reflecting that after
the development of my new theme it was appropriate to examine   5
the subject of Love, and also to please my friend, I decided to
write on this question. Then it was I wrote the sonnet which
begins: *Love and the noble heart* . . .

> Love and the noble heart are but one thing,
>   Even as the wise man tells us in his rhyme,
>   The one without the other venturing
>   No more than reason from a reasoning mind.
>   Nature, disposed to love, creates Love king,
>   Making the heart a dwelling-place for him
>   Wherein he lies quiescent, slumbering
>   Sometimes a little, now a longer time.
> Then beauty in a virtuous woman's face
>   Pleases the eyes, striking the heart so deep
>   A yearning for the pleasing thing may rise.
>   Sometimes so long it lingers in that place
>   Love's spirit is awakened from his sleep.
>   By a worthy man a woman's moved likewise.

This sonnet is divided into two parts. In the first I speak of Love
as he is in potentiality; in the second I speak of him as potentiality   10
made actual. The second part begins: *Then beauty* . . . The first
part is further divided into two sections. In the first I say in what
subject this potentiality resides; in the second I say how the
subject and potentiality are brought together to produce one
being and I describe how the one is in relation to the other as   15
form is to matter. The second subsection begins: *Nature, dis-
posed to love* . . . Next, where I say *Then beauty* . . . I say how
this potentiality is made actual, first in a man and secondly in a
woman, in the line: *By a worthy man* . . .

XXI

1 When I had discussed the nature of Love in the preceding rhyme,
I felt the desire to compose again; this time it was to be something
in which while praising my lady I should make plain how Love
is awakened through her, and not only awakened where he is
5 sleeping, for where he is not in potentiality she, by her miracu-
lous power, causes him to be. So then I wrote this sonnet which
begins: *Love is encompassed* . . .

Love is encompassed in my Lady's eyes
Whence she ennobles all she looks upon.
Where e'er she walks, the gaze of everyone
She draws; in him she greets, such tremors rise,
All pale, he turns his face away, and sighs,
Reflecting on his failings, one by one.
Fleeing before her, wrath and pride are gone.
Come, ladies, sing with me her eulogies,
All gentleness and all humility
When she is heard to speak in hearts unfold,
And blessed is he by whom she first was seen.
When she a little smiles, her aspect then
No tongue can tell, no memory can hold,
So rare and strange a miracle is she.

This sonnet has three parts. In the first I say how my lady
changes what is potential into act by the most noble power of
10 her eyes; and in the third I say how she does the same, by the
most noble power of her mouth; between these two parts is
another very short one which serves as an appeal for assistance
in moving from the preceding to the following; it begins: *Come,
ladies, sing* . . . and the third part begins: *All gentleness* . . . The
15 first of these principal parts is divided into three sections. In the
first I speak of her miraculous power of ennobling everything
she sees, and this amounts to saying that she calls Love into
potentiality where he is not; in the second I say how she actual-
izes Love in the hearts of all whom she sees; in the third I

describe the subsequent effects of her miraculous power over   20
their hearts. The second of these sections begins: *Where e'er she
walks* . . . ; the third: . . . *in him she greets* . . . Then where I say:
Come, ladies, sing . . . I make it clear to whom I mean to speak,
calling on other women to help me to do her honour. Then,
where I say: *All gentleness* . . . I repeat what is said in the first   25
part with reference to two actions of her mouth, one of which
is her sweetest utterance and the other her smile which stirs such
wonder; but what effect her smile has in people's hearts I do not
say because memory cannot retain it nor its operation.

XXII

Not many days after that, as it pleased the Lord of glory who   1
Himself experienced death, he who had been the father of this
wonder which Beatrice was seen to be, departing from our life,
passed truly to eternal glory. Such departure is always grievous
to friends who are left, and no friendship is so intimate as that   5
between a good father and a good child; and since my lady was
of the highest degree of goodness, and her father, as many
people believe and as is true, was also a man of great goodness,
it is plain that my lady was filled with bitterest sorrow. Since it
is the custom in the city I have mentioned for women to fore-   10
gather with women and men with men on such sad occasions,
a number of women met together where Beatrice was weeping
piteously. And I, seeing some of them returning, heard them
talking about her, saying how she mourned. Among their words
I was able to make out the following: 'She weeps so much that   15
truly anyone seeing her must die of compassion.' Then they
passed on and I was left in such distress that my face was bathed
in tears, and I hid my eyes in my hands again and again. I would
have hidden myself away at once as soon as my tears began to
flow, but I hoped to hear more about my lady, for where I was   20
most of the women would pass by as they took their leave of
her. So I remained in my place and other women passed by,
talking about her; and I heard them say: 'How can any of us

ever feel happy again after hearing her piteous words?' After
25 them came other women, saying: 'This man here weeps as
though he had seen her as we have.' And still others said concern-
ing me: 'Look at this man. You would hardly know him, he is
so changed!' In this way, as these women passed, I heard things
about my lady and myself, as I have related. Afterwards, think-
30 ing the matter over, I decided, as this was a suitable theme, to
put into verse what I had heard these women say. And since I
should have liked to question them, if it had not been out of
place, I arranged my material as if I had done so and as if they
had answered me. I composed two sonnets about it. In the first
35 I ask the questions I wanted to ask; in the other I give the
women's reply, based on what I heard them say, as if they had
answered me. I began the first sonnet with the words: *You who
approach* . . . ; and the second: *Are you that person* . . .

> You who approach, in aspect so cast down,
>   And by your lowered gaze your sadness prove,
>   Whence do you come, that all the colour of
>   Your cheeks has turned, it seems, to Pity's own?
> Our gentle lady have you looked upon,
>   Bathing with tears the countenance of Love?
>   Say to me, ladies, what your every move,
>   Ennobled by her, to my heart makes known.
> Coming from sorrow of such gravity,
>   With me, I pray, a little while remain,
>   And what befalls her do not keep from me.
> The marks of weeping in your eyes are plain,
>   And so transfigured you return I see,
>   My heart is shaken even by such pain.

This sonnet is divided into two parts. In the first I address the
40 women and ask them if they come from my lady, telling them
that I believe they do since they seem enhanced in graciousness;
in the second I entreat them to speak to me of her. The second
part begins: *Coming from sorrow* . . .

> Are you that person who so often spoke
>   About our lady, and to us alone?
>   Your voice indeed resembles his in tone
>   But in your face we find another's look.
>   Why do you weep so bitterly that folk
>   Are moved as though your sadness were their own?
>   Did you our lady weeping come upon
>   So that your inward grief you cannot cloak?
> Leave us to weep and mournful wend our way,
>   (To seek to comfort us would be a sin)
>   Recalling what in tears we heard her say.
>   So close does Pity to her visage cling
>   Whoever in her presence wished to stay
>   And gazed at her, had died of sorrowing.

This sonnet has four parts, in accordance with the four different ways of speaking of the women for whom I reply; and as they are set out plainly above, I will not undertake to relate the content of these parts, but merely indicate where divisions occur. The second part begins: *Why do you weep . . .* ; the third: *Leave us to weep . . .* ; and the fourth: *So close does Pity . . .*

XXIII

A few days after this, it happened that a painful illness affected a certain part of my body which caused me intense pain for nine days on end. This made me so weak that I lay like someone paralysed. On the ninth day, in the midst of almost unendurable pain, a thought came to me concerning my lady. And when I had thought about her for a little while, I fell to thinking about my own life, now so debilitated, and reflecting how short this life is, even in health, I began to weep about our wretched state. Sighing deeply, I said to myself: 'One day, inevitably, even your most gracious Beatrice must die.' This thought threw me into such a state of bewilderment that I closed my eyes, and I began, like a person who is delirious, to be tormented by these fantasies.

First, as my mind began to wander, I saw faces of dishevelled
women, who said: 'You too will die.' And then, after these
women, other faces appeared, strange and horrible to look at,
saying: 'You are dead.' Then, my imagination still wandering, I
came to some place I did not know, where I saw women going
about the street, weeping and in disarray, in terrible distress. I
seemed to see the sun grow dark and stars turn to such a colour
that I thought they were weeping; birds flying in the air fell
dead, and the earth trembled with great violence. As I marvelled
in my fantasy, growing very much afraid, I thought that a friend
came to me and said: 'Do you not know? Your wonderful lady
has departed from this world.' Then I began to weep most
piteously, and I wept not only in my dreams but with my eyes,
which were wet with real tears. I thought I was looking up
into the heavens, where I seemed to see a multitude of angels
returning to their realm, and before them floated a little cloud
of purest white. The angels were singing to the glory of God
and the words I seemed to hear were: *Osanna in excelsis*,[1] and
that was all I could make out. Then my heart, which was so full
of love, said to me: 'It is true that our lady is lying dead.' And
when I heard this, I seemed to go to see the body in which that
most noble and blessed soul had been; and the illusion was so
powerful that I saw my lady lying dead, and women seemed to
be covering her, that is, her head, with a white veil. On her face
was such an expression of serenity that she seemed to say: 'I
now behold the fountainhead of peace.' In my dream I was filled
with such serenity at the sight of her that I called on Death and
said: 'Sweet Death, come to me; do not be cruel to me, for you
must now have grown gracious after being in such a presence!
Come now to me, for I greatly desire you; see, I already wear
your colour!' When I had seen all the sorrowful necessities
completed which it is customary to perform for the bodies of
the dead, I thought that I returned to my room; there I looked
up towards Heaven and so vivid was my fantasy that as I wept
I began to say in my real voice: 'O most beautiful soul, how
blessed is he who beholds you!' As I was sobbing out these

1. Hosannah in the highest.

words and calling on Death to come to me, a kind and gentle
young woman who was standing beside my bed, thinking my   50
tears and cries were caused solely by the pain of my illness,
began to weep herself, in great alarm. Whereupon, other women
who were present in the bedroom noticed that I was weeping
by the distress which it was causing her. Sending away from my
bedside this young woman, who was closely related to me, they   55
drew near to arouse me, thinking I was dreaming, and said:
'Sleep no longer' and 'Do not be distressed'. And as they spoke,
my vivid dream was broken just at the moment when I was
about to say: 'O Beatrice, blessed are you!' I had already uttered
the words 'O Beatrice' when I opened my eyes with a start and   60
realized I had been dreaming. And though I did utter her name,
my voice was so broken by my sobs that I had the impression that
no one understood. I felt very much abashed, but in response to
Love's prompting, I turned my face towards the women. When
they saw me, they began to say: 'He looks as if he were dead.'   65
And they said to each other: 'Let us see if we can rally him.' So
they said many things to reassure me and kept asking what had
frightened me. When I felt a little comforted, realizing it had all
been a dream, I answered: 'I will tell you what happened to me,'
and so I told them what I had seen from beginning to end,   70
keeping back only the name of my most gracious lady. Later,
when I had recovered from my illness, I decided to write some
verses about what I had experienced, as it seemed appropriate
as a love-theme. So I wrote this *canzone* which begins: *A lady,
youthful* . . . , the arrangement of which is made clear in the   75
analysis which follows.

> A lady, youthful and compassionate,
>   Much graced with qualities of gentleness,
>   Who where I called on Death was standing near,
>   Beholding in my eyes my grievous state,
>   And hearing babbled words of emptiness,
>   Began to weep aloud in sudden fear.
>   And other women, being made aware
>   Of my condition by the one who cried,
>   Dismissed her from my side,

And drew, to rally me, about my bed.
'Wake from your sleep,' one said;
And one: 'What has bereft you of all cheer?'
My strange illusion then I put aside,
Calling the name of her for whom I sighed.

My voice, by grief made weak, so softly came,
So broken by the sobs which anguished me,
Only my heart her name could understand.
Despite my aspect all imbued with shame,
Which in my countenance was plain to see
I turned towards them at my Lord's command.
When they then saw me, of all colour drained,
They spoke as if they feared that I was dead.
'Oh, help him in his need!'
Gently they urged each other to the task,
And often they would ask:
'What did you see that left you so unmanned?'
Then when I was a little comforted
'Ladies, to you I'll speak of it,' I said.

'As thinking of my frail life I lay
And how its brief duration is as naught,
Love, dwelling in my heart, began to grieve;
At which my soul was filled with such dismay
That, sighing, I lamented in my thought:
"My lady, too, one day this life must leave."
Such desolation then my mind did cleave
I closed my eyes, lost in despondency.
In their perplexity
My spirits scattered and went wandering.
Then vain imagining,
Far from all truth, such as wild fancies weave,
Showed women's faces looming angrily,
Repeating "Die! You too, you too will die!"''

    'Then many fearful things my eyes did greet
       In the delusive dream which held me fast.
       I seemed to be – the place I did not know –
       Where women all dishevelled in the street,
       Some shedding tears, and others wailing, passed.
       Like fiery arrows flew their words of woe.
       Across the sun a darkness seemed to grow.
       The stars came out and from their heavenly wold
       They dropped tears, as of old.
       Birds flying in the air fell dead; earth shook;
       And with a pallid look
       A man appeared and to me whispered low:
       "What are you doing? Have you not been told?
       Your lovely lady's lying dead and cold."'

    'My eyes, with tears suffused, to heaven lifting,
       I saw, appearing like a shower of manna,
       Angels returning to the realms above.
       Ahead of them a little cloud was drifting,
       And as they followed it all cried *Hosanna*:
       No more they sang than this I tell you of.
       Then to reveal the mystery came Love,
       Saying to me, "Our lady come and see."
       Still in my fantasy,
       He brought me where I saw her lying dead,
       And gathered round her bed
       Women I saw who veiled her in a robe.
       With her, in truth, was such humility
       She seemed to say, "Peace has been granted me."'

    'Sorrow induced in me such humbleness,
       When all humility in her I'd seen,
       That I could say, "Sweet Death, I'll cherish thee,
       For thou art now a thing of graciousness
       Since in my lady's bosom thou hast been,

And wilt compassionate, not cruel, be.
So much I long to join thy company
That, see, already death-like I appear
And my heart bids: draw near."
Then I departed, every sad rite done,
And when I was alone,
Looking on high, I said: "Blessèd is he,
Fair soul, who may your goodness gaze upon."
Then at your words I woke, my vision flown.'

This *canzone* has two parts. In the first I relate, addressing an undefined person, how I was aroused from a delusion by certain women and how I promised to tell them about it; in the second
80 I give an account of what I told them. The second part begins: *As thinking of my frail life . . .* The first of these parts subdivides into two sections. In the first I say what the women, one of them in particular, said and did because of my fantasy, before I had come to myself; in the second I relate what they said when I had
85 awakened from my delirium; this section begins: *My voice, by grief made weak . . .* Then, where I say: *As thinking of my frail life . . .* I relate my dream as I told it to them, and this part is also subdivided into sections. In the first I relate the dream in the order in which it occurred; in the second, saying at what
90 moment the women aroused me, I express, indirectly, my gratitude to them. This section begins: *Then at your words . . .*

XXIV

1 After this delirious dream, it happened one day that as I was sitting thoughtfully by myself I felt a tremor in my heart as though I were in my lady's presence. Then a vision of Love came to me. He seemed to come from the direction where my lady
5 lived, and with great joy he said to me in my heart: 'Bless now the day I took you in my power for this you must surely do.' And indeed my heart seemed so full of joy that I did not know it for my heart in this unusual state. Soon after these words

which my heart spoke to me with the tongue of Love, I saw
approaching me a gracious lady, renowned for her beauty, who   10
for a long time had been the beloved of my closest friend. Her
name was Giovanna, but some say that because of her beauty
she was nicknamed Primavera, that is, Spring, and this is what
she was usually called. And coming after her, as I looked, I saw
the miraculous Beatrice. They passed by quite close to me, one   15
behind the other, and Love seemed to say to me in my heart:
'The first is called Primavera, and the sole reason for this is the
way you see her walking today, for I inspired him who gave her
this name of Primavera, which means that she will come first
(*prima verrà*) on the day Beatrice appears after the dream of the 20
one who serves her faithfully. If you also consider her first name,
it too signifies "she will come first", for Joan comes from John,
who preceded the True Light, saying *Ego vox clamantis in
deserto: parate viam Domini*.'[1] And afterwards Love seemed
also to say these words: 'Anyone who thought carefully about   25
this would call Beatrice Love because of the great resemblance
she bears to me!' Thinking about this later, I decided to compose
some verses for my best-loved friend, keeping back certain
words which it seemed better not to reveal, for I believed that
his heart was still in thrall to the beauty of this gracious Prima- 30
vera; and I wrote this sonnet which begins: *A spirit in my
heart* . . .

> A spirit in my heart which sleeping lay,
>   Being for love created, woke and stirred;
>   And from afar came Love himself, so gay,
>   That scarcely knowing him I thought I erred.
>   'You must take heed to honour me today,'
>   He said, smiling with joy at every word.
>   While he remained with me, I scanned the way
>   In the direction whence had come my Lord,
> And saw two whom their friends call Joan and Bee
>   Draw near the place where I stood wondering.

1.   I am a voice crying in the wilderness: prepare ye the way of the Lord. (cf.
     Matthew, iii, 3.)

> One miracle after another came!
> Love's words re-echo in my memory:
> 'She who precedes the other is called Spring,
> And she who is my image has my name.'

This sonnet has many parts; in the first I relate how I felt a familiar tremor in my heart and how Love seemed suddenly to
35 be there, happy in my heart, having come from far away; the second relates what Love seemed to say to me in my heart, and how he looked; the third relates how, when he had been with me a little while, I saw and heard certain things. The second part begins: *You must take heed . . .*; and the third: *While he*
40 *remained . . .* This third part is also divided into two: in the first section I say what I saw; in the second I say what I heard. The second section begins: *She who precedes . . .*

XXV

1 At this point someone whose objections are worthy of the fullest attention might be mystified by the way I speak of love as though it were a thing in itself, and not only a substance endowed with understanding but also a physical substance, which is
5 demonstrably false; for love is not in itself a substance at all, but an accident in a substance. That I speak of love as if it were a bodily thing, and even as if it were a man, appears from these three instances: I say that I saw him coming; now since 'to come' implies locomotion and, according to the Philosopher, only a
10 body in its own power is capable of motion from place to place, it follows that I classify love as a body. I say also that he laughed and that he spoke, which things are appropriate to a man, especially the capacity to laugh; and so it follows that I make love out to be a man. To clarify this matter, in a manner that is
15 useful to the present purpose, it should first be understood that in ancient times the theme of love was not taken as a subject for verses in the vernacular but there were authors who wrote on

love, namely, certain poets who composed in Latin; this means
that among us (and no doubt it happened and still happens in
other countries, as in Greece) those who wrote of love were not   20
vernacular but learned poets. It is not very many years ago
since the first vernacular poets appeared. I say poets because
composing rhymes in the vernacular is not so different from
writing verses in Latin, due proportion being borne in mind.
That it is not long ago that this happened can be shown to be   25
the case if we study the literature of the *langue d'oc* and of the
lingua del sì, for there is nothing written in these languages
earlier than one hundred and fifty years ago. The reason why a
few unpolished writers achieved the reputation of being able to
versify is that they were almost the first to write poetry in the   30
lingua del sì. The first to write as a vernacular poet was moved
to do so because he wished to make his verses intelligible to a
lady who found it difficult to understand Latin. This is an
argument against those who compose in rhyme on themes other
than love, because this manner of composition was invented   35
from the beginning for the purpose of writing of love. It follows
that since greater licence is granted to poets than to writers of
prose, and since those who write in rhyme are none other than
poets who write in the vernacular, it is reasonable and fitting
that greater licence should be granted to them than to others   40
writing in the vernacular; therefore if any figure of speech or
rhetorical colour is permitted to Latin poets it is permitted also
to those who write in rhyme. Thus if we see the ancient poets
spoke of inanimate things as if they had sense and reason, and
made them talk to each other, and that they did this not only   45
with real things but also with things which are not real, making
things which do not exist speak, and making accidents speak as
if they were substances and men, then it is appropriate for
someone writing in rhyme to do the same; not, of course, with-
out some justification, but with a reason that can be later made   50
clear in prose. That Latin poets have written in the manner
described may be seen by the example of Virgil who says that
Juno, a goddess who was hostile to the Trojans, spoke to Aeolus,
god of the winds, in the first book of the *Aeneid: Aeole, namque*

55 *tibi*,[1] and that he replied to her: *Tuus, o Regina, quid optes,*
explorare labor: mihi jussa capessere fas est.[2] In the words of
this same poet an inanimate thing speaks to animate things, in
the third book of the *Aeneid: Dardanidae duri.*[3] In Lucan an
animate thing speaks to an inanimate: *Multum, Roma, tamen,*
60 *debes civilibus armis;*[4] in Horace a man speaks to his own
learning, as though to a person; and not only are they words of
Horace, but he gives them as a quotation from the good Homer,
in his *Poetics: Dic mihi, Musa, virum.*[5] In Ovid, love speaks as
though it were a human being, at the beginning of his book
65 entitled *De Remedia Amoris*, where he says: *Bella mihi, video,*
bella parantur, ait.[6] This should serve as an explanation to
anyone who has doubts concerning any part of this little book
of mine. And lest any uneducated person should assume too
much, I will add that the Latin poets did not write in this manner
70 without good reason, nor should those who compose in rhyme,
if they cannot justify what they say; for it would be a disgrace if
someone composing in rhyme introduced a figure of speech or
rhetorical ornament, and then on being asked could not divest
his words of such covering so as to reveal a true meaning. My
75 most intimate friend and I know quite a number who compose
rhymes in this stupid manner.

1. It was to you, Aeolus, that . . . (*Aeneid*, 1, 65).
2. It is for you, O Queen, and for no one else, to decide what you wish to be
    done; my duty is to carry out your orders (ibid., 1, 76–7).
3. You rough Trojans (Apollo's oracle is speaking; ibid., III, 94).
4. For all that, Rome, you have profited greatly from the civil wars (*Pharsalia*,
    1, 44). Dante was here following a corrupt text. Lucan is addressing Nero,
    not Rome, and the verb should be *debet*, not *debes*, the meaning being,
    'For all that, Rome has profited greatly from the civil wars.'
5. Tell me, my Muse, about the man . . . (*De Arte Poetica*, 141).
6. 'Some fine things, I see, some really fine things are being cooked up here,'
    said he. (*Remedia Amoris*, 1, 2.)

XXVI

This most gracious lady, of whom I have spoken in words   1
preceding the above, found such favour that when she walked
down the street people ran to see her; and this filled me with a
wonderful happiness. When she was near anyone such reverence
possessed his heart that he did not dare to raise his eyes nor to   5
respond to her greeting. Many people, having experienced this,
could bear witness to this for me, if anyone did not believe it.
Crowned and clothed with humility, she would go her way,
displaying no pride at what she saw and heard. Often people
said, when she had passed: 'This is no woman; this is one of the   10
fairest angels of Heaven.' And others said: 'She is a miracle;
blessed be the Lord who can create such marvels!' I say in truth
that she appeared so gracious and in every way so pleasing that
those who looked at her experienced in themselves a sweetness
so pure and gentle that they were unable to describe it; and there   15
was no one who could look at her without immediately sighing.
These and more marvellous things resulted from her influence.
Thinking about this, and wanting to resume the theme of her
praise, I decided to compose something that would convey the
marvellous and beneficent effects of her power, so that not only   20
those who could see her with their own eyes but others also
might know of her what words are able to convey. I then wrote
this sonnet which begins: *So deeply to be reverenced . . .*

> So deeply to be reverenced, so fair,
>   My lady is when she her smile bestows,
>   All sound of speaking falters to a close
>   And eyes which would behold her do not dare.
>   Of praises sung of her she is aware,
>   Yet clad in sweet humility she goes.
>   A thing from Heaven sent, to all she shows
>   A miracle in which the world may share.
> Her beauty entering the beholder's eye
>   Brings sweetness to the heart, all sweets above:

> None comprehends who does not know this state;
> And from her lips there seems to emanate
> A gentle spirit, full of tender love,
> Which to the soul enraptured whispers: 'Sigh!'

This sonnet is so simple to understand from what is related
above that it does not require any analysis. Therefore, leaving
it, I go on to say that my lady gained such favour that not only
was she honoured and praised, but because of her many other
women also were honoured and praised. When I observed this
I wished to draw it to the notice of those who had not seen it,
so I decided to compose something else to convey it. I then wrote
this other sonnet beginning: *They see all goodness* . . . which
tells how her influence affected other women, as will appear
from its division.

> They see all goodness perfect made who see
> My lady among ladies take her place.
> Her presence brings them such felicity
> They render thanks to God for this sweet grace.
> Her beauty has such wondrous quality
> It leaves in women's hearts no envious trace;
> Clothed in nobility they're seen to be
> Who walk with her, and faith and love embrace.
> The sight of her is humbling to all things.
> Such loveliness is not to her confined,
> For honoured her companions are thereby.
> To all she does a noble grace she brings.
> No one there is who, calling her to mind,
> Lost in Love's very sweetness does not sigh.

This sonnet has three parts. In the first I say among whom my
lady seemed most wonderful; in the second I say what a gift of
grace was her company; in the third I speak of the things she
miraculously brought about in others. The second part begins:
Her presence brings . . . ; the third: *Her beauty has* . . . This last
part is subdivided into three sections. In the first I say what she
brought about in women, that is, as to themselves; in the second

I say what she brought about in them in the eyes of others; in the third I show how not only in women but in everyone, and not only by her presence but in the remembrance of her she had a miraculous influence. The second section begins: *The sight of her* . . . ; and the third: *To all she does* . . .   45

XXVII

After this I began to reflect one day on what I had written   1
concerning my lady, that is, in the two preceding sonnets; and, realizing that I had not spoken of the effect she was bringing about in me at the present time, I felt that I had expressed myself inadequately. So I decided to say in rhyme how susceptible   5
I was to her influence and how her power affected me. As I thought I could not relate this in the brief span of a sonnet, I began a *canzone*, of which the first words are: *So long have I been* . . .

> So long have I been subject to Love's sway
>   And grown accustomed to his mastery
>   That where at first his rule seemed harsh to me
> Sweet is his presence in my heart today.
> Thus when all fortitude he takes away,
>   So that my frail spirits seem to flee,
>   Then I am lost in sweetness utterly
> And pallid looks my fainting soul display.
> Love marshals then against me all his might;
>   Routed, my spirits wander, murmuring,
>   And to my lady bring
> Petition for new solace in my plight.
> Thus by her merest glance I am unmanned,
> And pride so humbled, none could understand.

XXVIII

1   *Quomodo sedet sola civitas plena populo! facta est quasi vidua
    domina gentium.*[1]

I was still composing this *canzone* and had completed the
stanza which I give above when the Lord of justice called this
5   most gracious lady to partake of glory under the banner of
the blessed Queen, the Virgin Mary, whose name was always
uttered in prayers of the utmost reverence by this blessed Beat-
rice. Although perhaps it would be pleasing at this point to
discuss her departure from us, it is not my intention to do so
10 here for three reasons: the first is that to do so does not form
part of the present subject, as can be seen on referring to the
preface which precedes this little book; the second is that even
if it were part of the present subject, no words of mine would
be adequate to treat the subject as it should be treated; the third
15 is that, even supposing that both the one and the other were not
the case, it is not fitting for me to discuss her departure because
in so doing I should be obliged to write in praise of myself,
which is reprehensible above all things. I therefore leave this
subject to be discussed by someone else. Nevertheless, since the
20 number nine has occurred over and over again in what I have
written, and this clearly could not happen without reason, and
since in her departure the number nine seemed to play an impor-
tant part, it is appropriate to say something about this as seems
relevant to my theme. Therefore, I will first say what part it
25 played in her departure, and then I shall suggest some reasons
why this number was so closely associated with her.

1.   How doth the city sit solitary, that was full of people! How is she become
     as a widow! (*The Lamentations of Jeremiah*, i, 1–2.)

XXIX

Now, according to the Arabian way of reckoning time, her most noble soul departed from us in the ninth hour of the ninth day of the month; according to the Syrian method, she died in the ninth month of the year, because the first month in that system is Tixryn the first, which we call October; and according to our way of reckoning, she departed this life in the year of our Christian era, that is of the years of Our Lord, in which the perfect number had been completed nine times in the century in which she had been placed in this world; for she was born a Christian of the thirteenth century. Why this number was so closely connected with her might be explained as follows. Since, according to Ptolemy and according to Christian truth, there are nine moving heavens, and according to common astrological opinion, these heavens affect the earth below according to their conjunctions, this number was associated with her to show that at her generation all nine of the moving heavens were in perfect conjunction one with the other. This is one reason. But, thinking more deeply and guided by infallible truth, I say that she herself was this number nine; I mean this as an analogy, as I will explain. The number three is the root of nine, because, independent of any other number, multiplied by itself alone, it makes nine, as we see quite plainly when we say three threes are nine; therefore, if three is the sole factor of nine, and the sole factor of miracles is three, that is, Father, Son and Holy Ghost, who are three and one, then this lady was accompanied by the number nine to convey that she was a nine, that is, a miracle, of which the root, that is, of the miracle, is nothing other than the miraculous Trinity itself. Perhaps a more subtle mind could find a still more subtle reason for it; but this is the one which I perceive and which pleases me the most.

XXX

1 After she had departed this life, the city of which I have spoken
was left as though widowed, despoiled of all good, and I, still
mourning in this city of desolation, wrote to the rulers of the
earth, telling them something of its condition, and taking as my
5 beginning the words of the prophet Jeremiah: *Quomodo sedet
sola civitas*.[1] I say this so that no one may be surprised that I
quote them above, like a heading to the new material that
follows. If anyone wished to reproach me because I do not here
quote the rest of my epistle, my excuse is that I intended from
10 the beginning to write only in the vernacular, and since the
words which follow those I have quoted are all in Latin it would
be contrary to my intention if I quoted them all. I am well aware,
too, that my closest friend, for whom I write this work, also
desired that I should write it entirely in the vernacular.

XXXI

1 When my eyes had shed tears for so long that they were no
longer able to relieve my sorrow, I felt I would like to give vent
to it by a sorrowful composition. And so I decided to write a
canzone in which, in the midst of my lamentation, I would speak
5 of her on whose account grief had so destroyed my soul. And I
set to work on a *canzone* which begins: *Tears of compassion
. . .* So that this *canzone* may seem the more widowed after its
conclusion I will divide it now before I transcribe it, and this
method I shall adopt from now on.

10   I say, then, that this mournful little *canzone* has three parts.
The first is the prelude; in the second I speak of my lady; in the
third I speak sorrowfully to the *canzone*. The second part begins:
Beatrice has gone . . . ; and the third: *My piteous song . . .* The

---

1.   How doth the city sit solitary!

first of these three main parts is subdivided into three sections. In the first I say why I am moved to write; in the second I say to whom I wish to address my words; in the third I say of whom I wish to write. The second begins: *And so, as I remember* . . . ; and the third: *I'll talk of her* . . . Then where I say: *Beatrice has gone* . . . I begin to speak of her; and of this part I make two sections. First I give the reason why she was taken from us; then I say how greatly people mourn her departure; this second section begins: *From the fair person* . . . This section again divides into three; in the first I say who does not weep for her; in the second I say who does weep; in the third I describe my own state. The second of these sections begins: *But he who seeks* . . . ; and the third: *Harsh is the torment* . . . Finally where I say: *My piteous song* . . . I address the *canzone*, indicating among which ladies it should go and take up its abode.

> Tears of compassion for my grieving heart
>   Such torment have inflicted on my eyes
>   That, having wept their fill, they can no more.
>   Thus, if I still would ease this aching smart,
>   Which step by step brings closer my demise,
>   Words must bring aid, as weeping did before.
>   And so, as I remember how of yore,
>   While yet my lady lived, I spoke with you,
>   My gentle ladies, now with you alone,
>   For I would speak with none
>   Save those endowed with noble hearts and true,
>   I'll talk of her with tears, for she is gone.
>   To Heaven she has suddenly departed,
>   And here are Love and I left broken-hearted.
>
> Beatrice has gone to Paradise on high
>   Among the angels in the realm of peace,
>   And you, ladies, she has left comfortless.
>   No quality of cold caused her to die,
>   Nor heat, as brings to others their release,
>   But only virtue and great gentleness.
>   For light, ascending from her lowliness,

So pierced the heavens with its radiance,
That God was moved to wonder at the same
And a sweet longing came
To summon to Him such benevolence;
And from on high He called her by her name,
Because our grievous life He saw to be
Unfit for such a noble thing as she.

From the fair person which on earth was hers
Her noble soul departed, full of grace,
To dwell in glory as befits her state.
Whoever speaks of her and sheds no tears,
His heart is stone, so evil and so base,
No living spirit there can penetrate.
He scarcely can her image contemplate
Whose lowly mind and churlish-heartedness
Preclude him from the deepest pangs of grief.
But he who seeks relief
In weeping and would die in his distress,
Of every consolation, like a thief,
Stripping his soul, is one who to his cost
Can clearly bring to mind all we have lost.

Harsh is the torment of each sighing breath
When thoughts recall to my despondent mind
The one for whom my grieving heart is rent;
And often while I'm pondering on Death
The colour leaves my cheeks, so sweet I find
Anticipation of his blandishment.
And sometimes when my thought is fixed intent
Such anguish pierces me on every side,
I start up with the pain by which I'm fraught,
And to such shame I'm brought
That from the company of all I hide.
Then in my solitude, I call, distraught,
On Beatrice, and say: 'Are *you* then dead?'
And while I call on her, I'm comforted.

With tears of sorrow and with tears of anguish
    My heart is wearied when I am alone;
    Any who heard with pity would be filled;
    And what this life has been wherein I languish
    Since to the world above my lady's flown,
    To tell it all no tongue is there so skilled.
    And so, my ladies, even if I willed
    I could not truly tell you how I fare,
    For by my cruel life of bitter woe
    I have been brought so low
    That on my deathly pallor all men stare
    Seeming to say: 'I leave you to your foe.'
    But whatsoe'er I am, my lady sees
    And from her mercy still I hope for ease.

My piteous song, now go, and mournfully
    Upon those ladies and young maidens wait
    To whom I sent, of late,
    Your sisters bringing messages of gladness;
    And you, who are the daughter of my sadness,
    Seek out their company, disconsolate.

XXXII

When this *canzone* had been composed, there came to visit me
someone who in the hierarchy of friendship stands immediately
after the first, and he was so closely related in kinship to my
lady now in glory that no one was closer. After speaking to me
a little while he asked me to compose something for a lady who
had died, disguising his words so that it seemed as if he were
talking of someone else who was also dead. Realizing he was
speaking only of our blessed departed one, I said I would do as
he requested. Thinking about the matter afterwards, I decided
to write a sonnet in which I would give some expression to my
grief and send it to this friend of mine, so that it would seem

that I had written it for him. So I wrote the following sonnet,
which begins: *Come, gentle hearts . . .*

It has two parts. In the first I call on Love's faithful followers
to hear me; in the second I speak of my wretched state. The
second part begins: *To the relief they bring . . .*

> Come, gentle hearts, have pity on my sighs
>   As mournful from my breast you hear them go.
>   To the relief they bring my life I owe
>   Since I should die of sorrow otherwise;
>   Without them, to make recompense, my eyes,
>   More often than I'd wish, alas!, would flow
>   To lessen by their tears the weight of woe
>   Which on my weeping spirit grievous lies.
> Many a time you'll hear them calling her,
>   My gentle lady, who from here was borne
>   Into a kingdom worthier than this
>   Of her great virtue; and our life in scorn
>   Sometimes they will revile, as though they were
>   The soul itself forsaken by its bliss.

XXXIII

When I had written this sonnet, thinking about the person to
whom I intended to give it as though I had written it for him, I
realized that this seemed a poor and bare service to pay to
someone so closely associated with my lady now in glory. So,
before giving him the sonnet, I wrote two stanzas of a *canzone*,
one truly for him and the other for myself, although they both
appear written for the same person to anyone who does not
observe carefully; but anyone who studies them closely sees
quite plainly that different people are speaking, since one does
not call her his lady, while the other does, as is evident. Then I
gave him the above sonnet and the following *canzone*, telling
him I had written them all for him. The *canzone* begins: *When
I recall . . .* It has two parts. In one, that is, in the first stanza, this

dear friend of mine and relative of hers makes his lamentation; in
the second stanza it is I who lament, that is, in the stanza   15
beginning: *Amid my sighing* ... Thus it is plain that in this
canzone two persons are lamenting, one as a brother, and the
other as Love's servant.

When I recall that nevermore, alas!,
    That lady I shall see
    On whose account I mourn with such dismay,
    My grieving thoughts about my heart amass
    Such sorrow that I say:
    'My soul, why dost thou not depart from me?
    The torments which perforce will burden thee
    Here in the world which hateful to thee grows
    My mind with fearful apprehension fill.'
    To Death then I appeal
    As to a sweet, beneficent repose:
    'Come now to me,' with so much love I cry
    That I am envious of all who die.
Amid my sighing is to be discerned
    A sound of plaintiveness
    Which calls on Death, lamenting ceaselessly.
    To him my every aspiration turned
    When in his cruelty
    He held my lady fast in his duress.
    For then the marvel of her loveliness
    To Heaven withdrew and to our sight was lost,
    Transformed to spiritual beauty there,
    Diffusing everywhere
    A light of love which greets the angel-host,
    Moving their intellect, so deep and wise,
    To wonderment, so full of grace it is.

XXXIV

1   When the day came that a year was completed since my lady
    had become a citizen of eternal life, I was thinking of her as I
    sat drawing an angel on some wooden boards. As I worked, I
    turned my head and saw standing beside me certain men to
5   whom respect was due. They were watching what I was doing
    and from what they later said they had been there some time
    before I noticed them. When I saw them I arose and, greeting
    them, I said: 'Someone was present in my mind just now and so
    I was lost in thought.' Then, when they had gone, I returned to
10 my work of drawing figures of angels and as I drew, there came
    to me the idea of composing some anniversary verses, to be
    addressed to those who had just visited me. So then I wrote the
    sonnet which begins: *Within my mind* . . . It has two beginnings.
    so I will divide it in two different ways.

15   The first version of this sonnet has three parts. In the first I
    say that my lady was already in my thoughts; in the second I say
    how Love influenced me on that account; in the third I speak
    of the effects of Love. The second part begins: *Love felt her
    presence* . . . ; the third: *Lamenting, from my bosom* . . . This
20 second part has two divisions. In one I say that all my sighs
    went forth lamenting; in the second I say that some spoke certain
    words different from the others. The second section begins: *But
    those that issued* . . . Now taking the second version of the
    sonnet, it is divided in the same way, except that in the first part
25 I say at what moment my lady came into my mind, while in the
    other I do not say this.

> Within my mind there had appeared to me
>   The gentle lady whom, by virtue of
>   Her perfect goodness, God enthroned above
>   In Mary's heaven of humility.
>
> Within my mind there had appeared to me
>   The gentle lady who is mourned by Love,
>   When you were hither drawn, by virtue of

Her perfect soul, my handiwork to see.
Love felt her presence in my mind as he
Within my ravaged heart began to move,
And, saying to my sighs, 'Go forth!', he drove
Them hence and they departed dismally.
Lamenting, from my bosom they were rent,
Forming a voice which often and again
Brings to my grieving eyes new tears of woe;
But those that issued with the greatest pain
Murmured 'O noble mind', as forth they went,
'You rose to Heaven this day a year ago.'

XXXV

Afterwards, for some time, because I was in a place where I   1
remembered days gone by, I became very pensive and filled with
such sorrowful thoughts that I took on an appearance of terrible
distress. Becoming aware of my condition, I raised my eyes to
see if anyone noticed it; and then I saw a gracious lady, young   5
and very beautiful, who was looking at me from a window so
compassionately, as it seemed from her appearance, that all pity
seemed to be gathered there in her. And so, because when
unhappy people see compassion in others they are more swiftly
moved to weep, as though stirred to pity for themselves, my   10
eyes began to fill with tears; then, afraid of revealing the wretch-
edness of my life, I withdrew from this lady's gaze. Later I said
to myself: 'It must surely be that in that kindest lady's company
there is the most noble love.' Thereupon I decided to write a
sonnet addressed to her and containing what I have told in this   15
account. As this account is perfectly clear I will not analyse the
sonnet. It begins: *These eyes of mine . . .*

These eyes of mine beheld the tenderness
    Which marked your features when you turned your gaze
    Upon my doleful bearing and the ways
    I many times assume in my distress.

I understood then that you fain would guess
 The nature of the dolour of my days;
 And so straightway I grew afraid to raise
 My eyes lest they reveal my abjectness.
And as I from your vision then withdrew
 The tears within my heart began to well,
 Where all was stirred to tumult by your sight;
 And to my soul I murmured in my plight:
 'With her indeed that self-same Love must dwell
 Who makes you go thus weeping as you do.'

XXXVI

1   From then on wherever this lady saw me her expression grew
compassionate and her face turned pale almost as though with
love, reminding me often of my most noble lady who was always
of a similar colouring. Often indeed when I could not weep or
5   give expression to my sorrow I used to go to see this compassion-
ate being, the very sight of whom seemed to draw the tears from
my eyes. And so I felt impelled again to compose lines addressed
to her, and I wrote this sonnet which begins: *No woman's
countenance* . . . Because of the foregoing account, it has no
10   need of analysis.

No woman's countenance has ever worn
 In such miraculous degree the hue
 Of love and pity's look, from yielding to
 The sight of gentle eyes or folk who mourn,
As does your own when I approach forlorn
 And with my grieving face for mercy sue.
 Such thoughts then come to mind because of you
 My heart with fear and suffering is torn.
My wasted eyes I find I cannot keep
 From gazing at you ever and again,
 For by a tearful longing they are led.

Beholding you then so augments their pain
They are consumed by their desire to weep,
Yet in your presence tears they cannot shed.

XXXVII

The sight of this lady had such an effect on me that my eyes   1
began to delight too much in seeing her, with the result that
often I grew angry in my heart and reviled myself greatly. And
often too I cursed the vanity of my eyes and said to them in my
thoughts: 'Once you moved to tears all who saw you by your   5
sorrowful condition; now it seems that you are ready to forget
all that because of this lady who gazes at you; she is not gazing
at you at all, except in so far as she is sad about the lady in glory
for whom you used to weep. But weep now all you can, for I will
remind you of her many times, accursed eyes, for never, this side   10
of death, ought your tears to have ceased!' When I had spoken
within myself to my eyes in this way, I was beset with deep sighs
of anguish. In order that this battle which was raging within me
should not remain locked within the breast of the wretch who
was experiencing it, I decided to write a sonnet and include in it a   15
description of this condition which filled me with such horror.
And so I wrote the sonnet beginning: *The bitter tears* . . .

It has two parts. In the first I speak to my eyes as my heart
spoke within me; in the second I remove a doubt, explaining
who it is who speaks in this way. The second part begins: *So*   20
speaks my heart . . . It could be divided further but this would
be superfluous because its meaning is made quite clear by the
preceding account.

'The bitter tears which never ceased to flow,
        O eyes of mine, while seasons came and went,
        As you have seen, moved others to lament
        And in their weeping their compassion show;
        But now I think you would forgetful grow

If I, for my part, should prove negligent
And every cause of this did not prevent,
Recalling her you mourned not long ago.
Your levity I contemplate with dread
So that in fear and trembling now I see
The face of one who holds you with her eyes.
While life endures you should not ever be
Inconstant to your lady who is dead.'
So speaks my heart, I hear, and then it sighs.

XXXVIII

1   The appearance of this lady wrought in me such a strange
condition that I often thought of her as of someone who pleased
me too much. My thoughts about her were as follows: 'This is
a gracious lady, beautiful, young and wise; perhaps she has
5   appeared by Love's will so that my life may know peace.' Often
I thought about her more lovingly so that my heart consented
to it, that is, to my loving thought. And when I had consented,
I reflected, as if moved by reason, and said to myself: 'Lord,
what is this thought that tries to console me in this base fashion
10   and barely lets me think of anything else?' Then another thought
rose up and said: 'You have recently been in great tribulation.
Why do you not want to escape from such bitterness? You see
that this is an inspiration of Love, who brings his desires before
us, and it proceeds from a most noble source as are the eyes of
15   the lady who has shown us such compassion.' Having battled
within myself in this manner many times, I decided to compose
some more verses on this subject; and since in the battle of my
thoughts those which supported the lady were victorious, it
seemed fitting to address myself to her; so I composed this
20   sonnet, which begins: *Thought which is gentle* . . . I call it gentle
because it spoke of a gentle lady; in all other respects it was
most base.

In this sonnet I divide myself into two parts, according to the
way in which my thoughts were divided. One part I call my

heart, that is, desire; the other I call my soul, that is, reason; and   25
I relate what they say to each other. That it is appropriate to
call desire the heart, and reason the soul is quite plain to those
to whom I wish the matter to be clear. It is true that in the
preceding sonnet I take the part of the heart against that of the
eyes, and that seems contrary to what I say in the present one.   30
Therefore I say that there also I mean the heart to signify desire
because my desire to remember my most gracious lady was still
greater than to see the new one, although I already had some
desire to do so, but it seemed slight. From this it is plain that the
one interpretation is not contrary to the other.   35

This sonnet has three parts. In the first I begin to tell this lady
how my desire turns wholly towards her; in the second I relate
how my soul, that is reason, speaks to the heart, that is desire;
in the third I give the heart's reply. The second begins: *The soul
then* . . . ; the third begins: *The heart replies* . . .   40

> Thought which is gentle, since it speaks of you,
>> Comes frequently to dwell with me a while.
>> Of love it reasons in so sweet a style
>> The heart is vanquished and consents thereto.
>> The soul then of the heart inquires, 'Pray, who
>> Is this who would our intellect beguile?
>> And is his virtue such as to exile
>> All other contemplation from our view?'
> The heart replies: 'O meditative soul,
>> This little spirit, newly sent by Love,
>> Its longings and desires before me brings.
>> Its life and power are emanations of
>> The glances of the Lady Pitiful
>> Who felt compassion for our sufferings.'

XXXIX

1 In opposition to this opponent of reason there rose up one
day within me, almost at the ninth hour, a vivid impression in
which I seemed to see Beatrice in glory, clothed in the crimson
garments in which she first appeared before my eyes; and she
5 seemed as young as when I first saw her. Then I began to think
about her and as I recalled her through the sequence of time
past my heart began to repent sorrowfully of the desire by which
it had so basely allowed itself to be possessed for some days
against the constancy of reason; and when this evil desire had
10 been expelled all my thoughts returned once more to their most
gracious Beatrice. And I say that from then onwards I began to
think of her so much with the whole of my remorseful heart
that frequently my sighs made this evident, expressing as they
issued what my heart was saying, that is, the name of this
15 most gracious soul and how she had departed from us. It often
happened that a thought would be so laden with grief that I
forgot what the thought had been and where I was. As a result
of the rekindling of my sighs, my weeping which had abated
was also refuelled to such an extent that my eyes were like two
20 objects desirous only of shedding tears; and it often happened,
because I wept for so long, that my eyes were ringed with dark
red, which happens as a result of some illnesses which people
suffer. Thus it seems that they were justly rewarded for their
inconstancy, so much so that from then onwards I could not
25 look at anyone who might return my gaze in such a way as to
cause my eyes to weep again. Then, as I wanted this evil desire
and vain temptation to be shown to be destroyed, so that the
verses I had written previously should raise no doubts in anyone,
I decided to write a sonnet to convey the substance of this
30 narration. So I then wrote: *Alas! by the violence of many sighs*.
I said 'Alas' because I was ashamed that my eyes had indulged
in such inconstancy.

I will not divide this sonnet because the foregoing account of
it makes it quite clear.

Alas! by the violence of many sighs
  Born of the thoughts I harbour in my breast,
  I cannot meet the gaze of others, lest
  I bring new torment to my vanquished eyes:
  Two orbs of longing now, their solace is
  To flow with tears and only grief attest.
  So much they weep that Love makes manifest
  An encircling crown which suffering implies.
These thoughts of mine and sighs which forth I send
  Within my heart to sharper anguish grow,
  Where Love in mortal pallor lies in pain;
  For in the deep recesses of their woe
  The sweet name of my Lady they have penned
  And many words to tell her death again.

XL

After this tribulation it happened, at the time when many people
go on pilgrimages to see the blessed image which Jesus Christ
has left us as an imprint of His most beautiful countenance,
which my lady in glory now sees, that some pilgrims were
passing along a road which runs almost through the centre of
the city where that most gracious lady was born, lived and died.
These pilgrims, it seemed to me, were very pensive as they went
their way; and so, thinking about them, I said to myself: 'These
people seem to be journeying from far away, and I do not think
they have ever even heard of my lady; they know nothing about
her, indeed their thoughts are on quite other things than those
that are around them here; perhaps they are thinking of their
friends at home, of whom we know nothing.' Then I said to
myself: 'I know that if they came from a nearby town they
would look distressed as they passed through this sorrowing
city.' Then I said: 'If I could detain them for a little while, I
would surely make them weep before they left, for I would say
things which would reduce to tears everyone who heard me.'
And so, when they had passed from my sight, I decided to write

20   a sonnet in which I would set forth what I said to myself; and
to make it more moving, I decided to write it as if I had spoken
to them. So I wrote the sonnet which begins: O *pilgrims* . . . I
called them pilgrims in the general sense of the word; for 'pil-
grim' may be understood in two ways, one general and one
25   particular, in as much as anyone journeying from his own
country is a pilgrim. In the particular sense, pilgrim means
someone who journeys to the sanctuary of St James and back.
It should be understood that those who travel in the service of
the Almighty are of three kinds. Those who travel overseas are
30   called palmers, as they often bring back palms; those who go to
St James's shrine in Galicia are called pilgrims, because the
burial place of St James was further away from his country than
that of any other apostle; and romeos are those who go to Rome,
which is where those whom I call pilgrims were going.
35   I do not divide this sonnet since it is quite clear from the
foregoing account.

> O pilgrims, meditating as you go,
>   On matters, it may be, not near at hand,
>   Have you then journeyed from so far a land,
>   As from your aspect one may plainly know,
>   That in the sorrowing city's midst you show
>   No sign of grief, but onward tearless wend,
>   Like people who, it seems, can understand
>   No part of all its grievous weight of woe?
> If you will stay to hear the tale unfold
>   My sighing heart does truly promise this:
>   That you will go forth weeping when I've done.
>   This city's lost her source of blessedness,
>   And even words which may of her be told
>   Have power to move tears in everyone.

XLI

Later two gracious ladies sent word to me, requesting me to   1
send them certain of my verses. Reflecting on their noble lineage,
I decided to send them a new composition, written specially for
them, together with those they had asked for, in order that I
might fulfil their request the more worthily. So I then wrote a   5
sonnet describing my state and sent it to them with the previous
sonnet and with another which begins: *Come, gentle hearts* . . .
   The sonnet which I wrote specially for them begins: *Beyond
the widest* . . . It is divided into five parts. In the first I say where
my thought goes, and I call it a sigh, naming it thus after one of   10
its effects; in the second I say why it ascends where it does, that
is, what causes it to ascend; in the third I say what it sees, that
is, a lady in glory; and then I call it a pilgrim spirit, for spiritually
it ascends into the heavens, and there abides for a while, like a
pilgrim who is away from his own country; in the fourth I say   15
that it sees her so beatified, that is, possessed of such attributes,
that I cannot comprehend, that is to say, my thought ascends so
far into the quality of her being that my intellect cannot follow
it; for our intellect in the presence of those blessed souls is as
weak as our eyes before the sun; and this is confirmed by the   20
Philosopher in the second book of his *Metaphysics*; in the fifth
part I say that although I cannot comprehend the place to which
my thought takes me, that is, into the presence of her miraculous
nature, I understand this at least, that this thought of mine is
entirely concerned with my lady, for frequently I hear her name.   25
At the end of this fifth part I say: 'Beloved ladies', to convey that
it is to ladies to whom I write these lines. The second part begins:
A new celestial; the third: *As it nears* . . . ; the fourth: *Gazing at
her* . . . ; and the fifth: *That noble one* . . .

> Beyond the widest of the circling spheres
>   A sigh which leaves my heart aspires to move.
>   A new celestial influence which Love
>   Bestows on it by virtue of his tears
>   Impels it ever upwards. As it nears

Its goal of longing in the realms above
The pilgrim spirit sees a vision of
A soul in glory whom the host reveres.
Gazing at her, it speaks of what it sees
In subtle words I do not comprehend
Within my heart forlorn which bids it tell.
That noble one is named, I apprehend,
For frequently it mentions Beatrice;
This much, beloved ladies, I know well.

XLII

1   After this sonnet there appeared to me a marvellous vision in
which I saw things which made me decide to write no more of
this blessed one until I could do so more worthily. And to this
end I apply myself as much as I can, as she indeed knows. Thus,
5   if it shall please Him by whom all things live that my life continue
for a few years, I hope to compose concerning her what has
never been written in rhyme of any woman. And then may it
please Him who is the Lord of courtesy that my soul may go to
see the glory of my lady, that is of the blessed Beatrice, who
10 now in glory beholds the face of Him *qui est per omnia secula
benedictus*.[1]

Beatrice compared to God

1. Who is blessed for ever.

Notes

II, 1: *the heaven of the light*: I.e. the heaven of the sun. According to pre-Copernican astronomy, the earth was the centre of the universe. Around it circled seven planets, of which the sun was the fourth. In separate concentric heavens, they were carried round the earth once every twenty-four hours. As well as this diurnal movement, each planet had an individual movement of its own. The sun, for instance, while revolving with the other six planets from east to west once every day and night, also revolved slowly from west to east, taking a solar year to complete this independent motion. By saying that the heaven of the sun had almost completed nine of its own circles since his birth, Dante indicates that he was almost nine years old when he first saw Beatrice (traditionally, in May 1274). See also Notes to XXIX, 13 and 14.

II, 4: *She was called Beatrice by many who did not know what it meant to call her this*: It is Boccaccio who first tells us that the Beatrice of the *Vita Nuova* and of the *Divina Commedia* was Beatrice dei Portinari of Florence, who married Simone dei Bardi and died in 1290. Dante's reference to her name in this passage is so ambiguous that some commentators consider that he means to convey that she was an abstract beneficent influence personified as a woman with the symbolic name of Beatrice ('she who blesses'). His words are here interpreted to mean that her name, Beatrice, suited her better than many knew who called her by it.

II, 6: *the heaven of the fixed stars*: Beyond the seven heavens containing the planets was an eighth heaven which carried the constellations. These were called 'fixed stars' because in comparison with the planets they appeared to have no independent motion. But the stars of the eighth heaven also, as well as revolving with the planets once every twenty-four hours round the earth, very slowly traced a course from west to east, taking 100 years to complete one degree, or 36,000 years to complete one circle. By saying that the heaven of the fixed stars had moved one-twelfth of a degree to the east since the birth of Beatrice, Dante indicates that she was eight years and four months old.

II, 13: *the vital spirit*: Dante follows Hugh of St Victor in identifying three principal forces of life in the body, which he calls spirits. The 'vital spirit' is the force which is centred in the heart. The 'spirit of the senses' is centred in the brain. The 'natural spirit' is centred in the liver. In addition to these three main forces, there are the senses, which Dante also personifies as spirits, attributing emotion and dialogue to them. (See chapter XI.)

II, 18: *the place to which all our sense perceptions are carried*: I.e. the brain.

II, 22: *where our nourishment is digested*: I.e. the liver.

II, 32: *the words of the poet Homer*: In the *Iliad*, Book XXIV, line 258, Priam says, speaking of Hector: 'He did not seem the son of mortal man, but of a god.' Dante, who knew no Greek, had read this in a Latin translation of Aristotle's *Ethics*, Book VII, chapter 1. He refers to this passage again in two later works, *Il Convivio* ('The Banquet') and *Monarchia* ('Monarchy'); in these instances it appears that Dante understands Aristotle to use this quotation from Homer in support of the belief that some human beings are so noble as to justify their being called divine. Of these, Beatrice is one.

II, 40: *omitting many things which might be copied from the master-text*: The 'master-text' is the 'book' of Dante's memory. It is not his intention to copy everything from it, nor even everything that comes under the first heading.

III, 1: *exactly nine years*: According to tradition, the meeting referred to here occurred in May 1283. Dante had often seen Beatrice in the interval (cf. chapter II) but this meeting, nine years after the first, appears to have had the quality of a revelation.

III, 1: *this gracious being*: The Italian word *gentile* has no adequate equivalent in English. 'Gentle' implies too little, and too much that is irrelevant. 'Gracious' will sometimes, but not always, serve. Similarly the word *donna* can sometimes be translated as 'lady', but in other contexts 'woman', 'being', or 'person' seems more appropriate.

III, 10: *the ninth hour of the day*: According to medieval reckoning, there were twelve day hours and twelve night hours; the day hours were those between sunrise and sunset, the night hours were those between sunset and sunrise. Twice a year, at the spring and autumn equinox, the hours of the day and the hours of the night were equal in length. With the advance of summer, the daylight hours increased in length, though still remaining twelve in number. After the summer solstice (21 June), the daylight hours became shorter and those of the night longer. Sunrise was reckoned as beginning at 6 a.m., the first hour of the day. At the spring equinox (21 March) the ninth hour of the day was 3 p.m. by our reckoning; in May it was nearer 4 p.m.

III, 11: *the first time she had ever spoken to me*: Dante must have heard her voice before, but it appears from this that she had not previously addressed him directly.

III, 17: *a lordly figure*: This is love personified.

III, 35: *a number of poets who were famous at that time*: Among the established poets who wrote in the vernacular were Guittone of Arezzo, Chiaro Davanzati, Bonagiunta of Lucca, Cino of Pistoia, Terino of Castelfiorentino, Dante of Maiano and Guido Cavalcanti.

III, 35: *As I had already tried my hand at the art of composing in rhyme*: Among Dante's early poems are five sonnets on the subject of love addressed to his namesake, Dante of Maiano. These were probably written when Dante was about seventeen years old.

III, 45: *replies from many*: Only three replies have been preserved, one from Dante of Maiano, one from Cino of Pistoia (or from Terino of Castelfiorentino) and one from Guido Cavalcanti.

III, 47: *my closest friend*: I.e. Guido Cavalcanti.

III, 49: *he learned that it was I who had sent him the sonnet*: It was the custom for young poets to send poems anonymously to others who were already established.

III, 50: *The true meaning ... is perfectly clear*: Dante here interprets the dream as a prophecy of the death of Beatrice. It is not known what interpretation he intended when he wrote the poem.

IV, 1: *my natural spirit*: See Note to chapter II, 13.

V, 1: *in a place where words about the Queen of glory were heard*: I.e. in a church, where words were spoken in praise of the Virgin.

V, 18: *a few little things for her in rhyme*: Among Dante's early love poems, addressed to other women than Beatrice, are several graceful and charming trifles, probably intended to be set to music.

V, 21: *apart from one*: This is the double sonnet beginning *O you who on the road of love pass by*.

VI, 7: *an epistle in the form of a serventese*: This has not been preserved. In Provençal literature a *serventese* was originally a homage poem, addressed to a feudal lord. It later came to be an exhortatory poem of praise or blame. In Italian, the form of the *serventese* was used for love poetry.

VII, 10: *O you who on the road of Love pass by*: This is a double sonnet, a form said to have been invented by Guittone of Arezzo. Only three double sonnets by Dante are known to us, two of which are contained in the *Vita Nuova*, this and the one beginning, *Death villainous and cruel*.

VII, 17: *beginning and end of the sonnet*: I.e. the first six and the last eight lines.

VIII, 8: *I touched on this in the last part*: I.e. in the last two lines of the sonnet beginning *Death villainous and cruel*.

VIII, 23: *a person left undefined, although defined in my own intention*: I.e. perhaps himself.

IX, 3: *travel in the direction of the region*: Where was Dante travelling? It has been suggested that he refers here to an expedition of the Florentine militia, which took part in the attack on Castel di Poggio di Santa Cecilia where a rebellion against the Guelf League had been instigated by the Ghibellines of Arezzo. This enterprise, begun in October 1285, lasted until April of the following year, when the castle surrendered.

IX, 8: *my source of happiness*: I.e. Beatrice.

IX, 13: *a beautiful stream of clearest water*: I.e. the Arno, at which Love gazes as though longing to follow its course to Florence.

X, 10: *departing somewhat from the immediate subject*: Dante's subject is his poetry and the events and feelings which inspired it. The following description of the effect on him of the greeting of Beatrice is 'somewhat' of a digression.

XI, 8: *a spirit of love, ... spirits of vision*: Dante here personifies his feeling and senses as though they were separate parts of his being. See also Note to chapter II, 13.

XII, 6: *the Lady of courtesy*: Probably the Virgin Mary, but some commentators think that Beatrice is intended. The word *cortesia* is used by Dante elsewhere to mean compassion, or grace. In chapter XLII, 8 God is called the 'Lord of courtesy'.

XII, 13: *Fili mi ... simulacra nostra*: The 'false images' are presumably the screen ladies to whom Dante has shown love in order to keep secret his love for Beatrice.

XII, 20: *Ego tanquam ... autem non sic*: Love seems here to be distinguishing between the general and the particular. Love in general is related to the whole of life and equally to all mankind. Love therefore weeps at the thought that Dante must now withdraw his love from the second screen-lady. In realistic terms, Dante feels a pang of regret on realizing that, though love is universal, he, an individual, cannot love diffusedly, but must love one and one only. He has reached the moment of choice, which for finite minds involves exclusion.

XII, 25: *'Do not ask more than is useful for you!'*: These words echo St Paul who in Romans xii, 3 bids us 'not to know more than it is meet to know, but to know in due measure'. Dante quotes them in *Il Convivio* IV, 13.

XII, 47: *the ninth hour of the day*: See Note to chapter III, 10.

XII, 60: *I intend to clarify and resolve this doubt later on in this little book*: Dante takes up the question of personification in poetry in chapter XXV.

XIII, 15: *Nomina sunt consequentia rerum*: This sentence may be derived from Roman law.

XIV, 3: *a friend*: It is not known who this friend was. According to laws governing weddings and funerals in Florence of Dante's time, each invited guest was entitled to bring a companion with him. A knight was entitled to bring four companions, a judge or a doctor, three. Dante, if he was the sole companion, was chosen by a guest who was not a knight, a judge or a doctor, but that is all we can deduce concerning him.

XIV, 4: *so many beautiful women*: Not more than twenty-five, including the bride, according to the same laws.

XIV, 7: *his friend*, i.e. Dante.

XIV, 12: *when she sat down at table*: The courses at weddings were limited to three, not counting fruit and sugared almonds.

XIV, 22: *Then my spirits . . .* : See Note to chapter II, 13.

XIV, 40: *'I had set foot . . . returning'*: I.e. he had been brought to the verge of death.

XV, 1: *After this strange transformation:* I.e. the experience he has undergone in the presence of Beatrice at the wedding.

XVII, 1: *these three sonnets*: Sonnets 7, 8 and 9 in which Dante describes the effect on him of the sight and thought of Beatrice.

XVII, 3: *I thought it right to be silent and say no more*: In the three sonnets to which he refers Dante considers he has said everything possible concerning the state of his mind and heart in relation to Beatrice. What he will write henceforth will be praise of her.

XIX, 2: *a stream of very clear water*: Commentators are divided in their views as to whether this is the stream mentioned in chapter IX. If so, it is the Arno. If not, it may be one of the many streams which watered the countryside near Florence.

XIX, **Canzone, stanza 2, 12–14**: *Where one knows he must lose her*

... *Heaven's blessed*: Dante is here probably referring to the possibility of his own damnation. There seems to be no valid reason for believing that the words 'and who will say in Hell' imply that Dante had already envisaged writing the *Inferno* at the time of the composition of this *canzone*. Similar allusions to Hell and to the poet's damnation, consoled by the memory of the beloved, are to be found in love poetry of the period and immediately preceding.

The contradiction between these lines and those concluding the third stanza ('With further grace has God endowed her still: Whoe'er did speak with her shall not fare ill') may perhaps be resolved by reading into the word 'spoke' ('*chi l'ha parlato*' in the original) a meaning of harmonious relationship, from which at the time of writing this *canzone* Dante feels himself excluded.

XIX, 38: *effective powers*: I.e. results of her nobility of soul.

XIX, 60: *if it should come to the ears of too many*: Dante did not intend to reveal the meaning of this poem to all and sundry. Compare the last stanza of the poem itself.

XX, 1: *When this canzone had circulated*: It was fairly well known by 1292.

XX, 2: *a friend*: Possibly Guido Cavalcanti, though he is usually referred to by Dante as his 'most intimate friend'.

XX **Sonnet, stanza 1, 2**: *the wise man*: This epithet (*il saggio*, in Italian) was commonly applied to poets in Dante's time. The poet referred to here is Guido Guinizelli.

XXIII, 1: *A few days after this*: I.e. a few days after the funeral. It is not known what Dante's illness was. It occurred evidently in the winter of 1290, Dante being then twenty-five. As a few days previously he had been out in the winter weather, weeping as he saw the mourners returning from the house of the Portinari, he may have succumbed to pleurisy or pneumonia. He seems, from the poem, to have had a high temperature and to have been in delirium.

XXIII, 55: *this young woman, who was closely related to me*: She is believed to be one of Dante's two step-sisters, born of his father's second marriage to Lapa di Chiarissimo Cialuffi. One, named Tana, married Lapo di Riccomanno Pannocchia. The other, whose Christian name is not known, married Leone di Poggio and had a son, Andrea, whom Boccaccio described as bearing a physical resemblance to Dante, from which we may deduce that Dante resembled his father more closely than his mother.

XXIII, 77: *addressing an undefined person*: I.e. in contrast to the first *canzone*, which is addressed to 'Ladies who know by insight what love is'.

XXIV, 10: *a gracious lady, renowned for her beauty*: This is Giovanna, the lady loved by Guido Cavalcanti.

XXIV, 15: *one behind the other*: In the narrow streets of Florence, with their even narrower footpaths, it is often impossible to walk two abreast.

XXIV, 18: *I inspired him who gave her this name*: I.e. Guido Cavalcanti, who gives Giovanna the name of Primavera in his poem, beginning *Fresca rosa novella, piacente Primavera* (O fresh, new rose, O pleasing Spring).

XXIV, 29: *for I believed that his heart was still in thrall*: Dante implies that Cavalcanti, at the time of the composition of the poem, would not have been pleased to hear Love's words concerning the symbolic relationship of Giovanna to Beatrice.

XXIV, **Sonnet, stanza 2**, 1: *Joan and Bee*: These are English equivalents of the Italian abbreviations *Vanna* and *Bice*, used by Dante in the poem. It is said that Beatrice dei Portinari was called Bice.

XXV, 3: *not only a substance endowed with understanding but also a physical substance*: In scholastic theology, a *substance* is a thing existing in itself; an *accident* resides in a *substance*, being, as we should now say, the *property* of a thing existing in itself. Thus grass is a substance, and greenness is an accident of that substance, it being the property of grass to be green. Love is not a substance but the property of substances (e.g. men capable of loving). Dante, personifying love, is treating an accident as a substance.

XXV, 9: *the Philosopher*: I.e. Aristotle.

XXV, 28: *one hundred and fifty years ago*: The *Vita Nuova* is believed to have been written in the 1290s. This would mean that Dante knew of no literature in the *langue d'oc* (Provençal) or in the *lingua del sì* (Italian) earlier than 1140. This is valid for Italian but not for Provençal.

XXV, 29: *few unpolished writers*: This may be an allusion to Giacomo of Lentino, Orbiciani of Lucca and Guittone of Arezzo.

XXV, 31: *The first to write*: Dante here leaves out of account earlier didactic and moralizing verse in Provençal and Italian.

XXV, 35: *this manner of composition*: I.e. writing rhymed verse in Italian.

XXV, 40: *others writing in the vernacular*: I.e. prose writers.

XXV, 67: *concerning any part of this little book*: Dante is referring to chapter XII in which he has promised to explain his reasons for the use of personification in his verses.

XXV, 74: *My most intimate friend*: I.e. Guido Cavalcanti, who has evidently discussed poetry with Dante at some length. See Introduction.

XXVI, 18: *wanting to resume the theme of her praise*: This theme had been interrupted by the death of Beatrice's father, on the occasion of which Dante had written the two sonnets included here, and by his illness, which inspired the second *canzone*. These poems, though they are inspired by Beatrice, are not specifically concerned with praise of her. The sonnet beginning 'A spirit in my heart' concerns an exalted vision of Beatrice in relation to Giovanna, but it appears that Dante does not regard it as belonging to those poems in which he treats of the 'new and nobler theme' announced in chapter XVII.

XXVIII, 1: *Quomodo sedet . . . gentium*: These are the first words of the Lamentations of Jeremiah. In chapter XXX Dante justifies their introduction here as standing 'like a heading to the new material that follows'. Like Jerusalem, Florence has tried the patience of God, who has withdrawn Beatrice from earth to Heaven.

XXVIII, 5: *under the banner of . . .* : I.e. in the company of souls who are near the Virgin. When Dante beholds Beatrice in glory in *Paradiso* he finds that she is seated in the third circle of the Heavenly Rose, beside Rachel, who sits below Eve, who sits below the Virgin.

XXVIII, 11: *the present subject*: I.e. the presentation and exposition of his poems.

XXVIII, 11: *the preface which precedes this little book*: Dante is, it may be supposed, referring to chapter I in which he has said that he intends to copy the words contained in the book of his memory, 'or if not all, at least their meaning'.

XXVIII, 19: *the number nine . . . in what I have written*: I.e. in chapters II, III, VI, VII and XXIII.

XXIX, 1: *according to the Arabian way of reckoning time*: Dante's knowledge of this was derived from the *Elementa astronomica* by Alfraganus.

XXIX, 2: *the ninth day of the month*: I.e. according to the Arabian reckoning, corresponding, in the month in question (June), to the nineteenth day, in our reckoning.

XXIX, 3: *according to the Syrian method*: See below.

XXIX, 3: *the ninth month of the year*: I.e. June, which is the sixth month according to the Roman reckoning. See below.

XXIX, 4: *the first month in that system is Tixryn the first, which we call October*: The following comparative table makes this passage clear:

	Syrian method		Roman method	
1.	Tixryn the first	corresponding to	October	(10)
2.	Tixryn the second		November	(11)
3.	Canon the first		December	(12)
4.	Canon the second		January	(1)
5.	Xubât		February	(2)
6.	Adâr		March	(3)
7.	Nisân		April	(4)
8.	Eijâr		May	(5)
9.	Hazirân		June	(6)
10.	Tamûz		July	(7)
11.	Ab		August	(8)
12.	Eilûl		September	(9)

XXIX, 7: *the perfect number . . . in this world*: The 'perfect' (or complete) number is 10. It had been completed nine times in the century in which Beatrice was born, i.e. she died in 1290, and on 19 June. (See above.) The year 1290 corresponds in Arabian reckoning to the year 689, which, according to our reckoning began on 14 January. The Arabian Giumâda, which corresponds to our June and July, began on 11 June. The ninth day of Giumâda was therefore the nineteenth of our June.

Dante has recourse to three calendars to identify the date of the death of Beatrice. This miraculously coincided in all three reckonings with the number 9 and also with the perfect number 10 in our reckoning.

XXIX, 12: *Ptolemy*: I.e. the astronomer. Dante had no direct knowledge of his works. He knew Alfraganus' compendium of them, *Almagest*. It is Aristotle who spoke of the nine moving heavens and Dante's source is St Thomas Aquinas who quotes from Aristotle's *De coelo et mundo*.

XXIX, 13: *nine moving heavens*: According to the system of Ptolemy, there are seven heavens which bear seven planets (the moon, Mercury, Venus, the sun, Mars, Jupiter, Saturn), one heaven which bears the fixed stars, and one, the Primum Mobile, which bears no planets or stars but imparts movement to the other eight. They circle the earth in an east-to-west motion every twenty-four hours.

XXIX, 14: *according to their conjunctions*: The seven planets travel along their spheres in an independent west-to-east movement, each circling the earth in this direction at a different rate. They therefore appear at different times of the year in different positions in relation to each other and in conjunction with different fixed stars, which move, in an independent west-to-east motion, only one degree every 100 years.

XXX, 9: *my epistle*: It has not been preserved.

XXX, 13: *my closest friend . . . in the vernacular*: I.e. Guido Cavalcanti, who appears to have been intimately concerned in the planning of this book. See Introduction.

XXXII, 2: *someone . . . no one was closer*: This is Beatrice's brother. Two of her brothers, Manetto and Ricovero, were adult in 1287 when their father made his will.

XXXII, 10: *some expression to my grief*: As the poem was commissioned, Dante could not give full expression to his own grief, since he wished it to convey the emotions of someone else.

XXXIV, 1: *a year was completed*: I.e. it was 19 June 1291.

XXXIV, 2: *as I sat drawing an angel on some wooden boards*: Leonardo Bruni relates in his biography that Dante was a competent artist. There are several other indications in Dante's writings of his knowledge of painting and sculpture.

XXXIV, 4: *certain men to whom respect was due*: Perhaps members of the Council of Florence; or possibly church dignitaries who might have commissioned the work he was doing.

XXXIV, 8: *'Someone was present in my mind'*: I.e. as he drew, he was thinking of Beatrice.

XXXIV, 10: *my work of drawing figures of angels*: His work seems to have been an extensive composition of figures of angels for he is drawing on several boards. It may have been intended for a church.

XXXIV, 13: *It has two beginnings*: Perhaps Dante had already begun the sonnet and had written the first four lines when the visit occurred, and he began again.

XXXV, 5: *a gracious lady*: This is the 'donna gentile' whose identity has been much disputed. In his philosophic treatise, *Il Convivio* (The Banquet), Dante maintains that she is the symbol of philosophy. See Introduction.

XXXIX, 1: *this opponent of reason*: I.e. the heart, thus personified in the preceding sonnet; not, of course, the lady herself.

XXXIX, 8: *for some days*: Dante perhaps means the days during which he has suffered turmoil in his thoughts (see preceding chapter). His enamourment of the 'donna gentile' obviously lasted more than some days. The prose of chapters XXXVIII and XXXIX suggests a torment of physical desire which is not conveyed in the preceding sonnet.

XXXIX, 22: *some illnesses which people suffer*: In cases of nephritis (kidney disease), red, puffy patches appear round the eyes, similar to the effect produced by excessive weeping.

XL, 1: *at the time when many people go on pilgrimages to see the blessed image*: I.e. probably in Easter week, when the veil of St Veronica was displayed at St Peter's. This relic, on which it was believed Christ's features were imprinted when Veronica wiped the blood and sweat from His face as He passed on His way to Calvary, is mentioned again by Dante in *Paradiso* (Canto XXXI, 103–8).

XL, 5: *a road which runs almost through the centre of the city*: I.e. probably the ancient Roman road, the present Via degli Strozzi, Via degli Speziali and the Corso. In this last quarter was the house of Folco dei Portinari, the father of Beatrice.

XL, 33: *romeos*: The Provençal word *romen* or *romien* was applied to pilgrims from the West travelling to the Holy Land. Later it was used of pilgrims travelling to, rather than from, Rome.

XLI, 2: *their noble lineage*: Dante, who took pride in being himself well-born, was susceptible to ancient lineage in others.

XLI, 7: *Come, gentle hearts*: I.e. the sonnet he wrote for the brother of Beatrice. See chapter XXXII.

XLI, 20: *the Philosopher*: I.e. Aristotle. The passage in the *Metaphysics* to which Dante refers is quoted by St Thomas Aquinas (Summa III, 45).

XLI, 26: *'Beloved ladies'*: Dante ends, as he began, the theme of praise of Beatrice by addressing his poetry to other women.

XLII, 1: *a marvellous vision*: This is perhaps a vision which led him to envisage Beatrice as the symbol she became in the *Divina Commedia*.

XLII, 7: *written in rhyme*: Dante uses the verb *dicere* (*dire*) to mean to 'write in rhyme'.

Index of First Lines of Poems

PENGUIN ⓟ CLASSICS

The Classics Publisher

'Penguin Classics, one of the world's greatest series' JOHN KEEGAN

'I have never been disappointed with the Penguin Classics. All I have read is a model of academic seriousness and provides the essential information to fully enjoy the master works that appear in its catalogue' MARIO VARGAS LLOSA

'Penguin and Classics are words that go together like horse and carriage or Mercedes and Benz. When I was a university teacher I always prescribed Penguin editions of classic novels for my courses: they have the best introductions, the most reliable notes, and the most carefully edited texts' DAVID LODGE

'Growing up in Bombay, expensive hardback books were beyond my means, but I could indulge my passion for reading at the roadside bookstalls that were well stocked with all the Penguin paperbacks ... Sometimes I would choose a book just because I was attracted by the cover, but so reliable was the Penguin imprimatur that I was never once disappointed by the contents.

Such access certainly broadened the scope of my reading, and perhaps it's no coincidence that so many Merchant Ivory films have been adapted from great novels, or that those novels are published by Penguin' ISMAIL MERCHANT

'You can't write, read, or live fully in the present without knowing the literature of the past. Penguin Classics opens the door to a treasure house of pure pleasure, books that have never been bettered, which are read again and again with increased delight' JOHN MORTIMER

CLICK ON A CLASSIC
www.penguinclassics.com

The world's greatest literature at your fingertips

Constantly updated information on over 1600 titles, from Icelandic sagas to ancient Indian epics, Russian drama to Italian romance, American greats to African masterpieces

•

The latest news on recent additions to the list, updated editions and specially commissioned translations

•

Original scholarly essays by leading writers: Elaine Showalter on Zola, Laurie R. King on Arthur Conan Doyle, Frank Kermode on Shakespeare, Lisa Appignanesi on Tolstoy

•

A wealth of background material, including biographies of every classic author from Aristotle to Zamyatin, plot synopses, readers' and teachers' guides, useful web links

•

Online desk and examination copy assistance for academics

•

Trivia quizzes, competitions, giveaways, news on forthcoming screen adaptations

•

eBooks available to download